BONNER VC

THE BIOGRAPHY OF GUS BONNER: VC AND MASTER MARINER.

SUE SATTERTHWAITE

THIS BOOK IS DEDICATED TO THE

OFFICERS AND MEN OF THE Q-SHIPS.

Published in 2008 by SR Print Management Company. Aldridge. WS9 8UY

British Library Cataloguing in Publication Data.
A catalogue record for this book is available from the British Library.

ISBN 978-0-9554840-1-8

Notes on the text.

Where quotes are used they are reproduced as they were originally written,
save for an occasional explanation which has been added in brackets.
The twenty-four hour clock is used throughout.
Full stops in abbreviations have been deliberately omitted.

www.bonnervc.co.uk

CONTENTS

ACKNOWLEDGEMENTS

Many people have given assistance or offered advice during my research for Gus' biography but to name them all would require a separate chapter. I will begin with an apology to anyone who has been omitted from the list which follows and I very much hope that everyone who has made a contribution, however small, knows how grateful I am.

I am indebted to members of Gus Bonner's family for allowing me access to their family photographs, letters and documents, particularly David Partridge, Penelope and David Buik, James Bonner and Stephen Bonner.

My husband David has proof-read several times, been my sounding board, put up with my moods when things weren't quite going to plan and never once complained about the enormous amount of time which I have spent on this wonderful project. His support has been invaluable.

I am very fortunate that my interest in military research has brought me into contact with two people who have made a very significant contribution to this book. David Baldwin, who is the secretary of the West Midland Branch of the Military Historical Society and Ken Wayman, author of the 'The True and Faithful Men. Pelsall Servicemen in the Great War 1914-1918' and 'Thank God I'm Trying to do My Little Bit. A Walsall Lad's Letters from the Trenches,' have been involved in the project from the start and have proof-read every chapter more than once. They have done me a great service by being honest about my work, suggesting other avenues of research and offering both encouragement and constructive suggestions for improvement. This has been done not just out of a sense of friendship but also because they are each committed to making sure that the enormous debt we owe to those who have served and serve their country in war is not forgotten. This book would have been a much poorer effort without their valuable contribution and I hope that they both know that I am very grateful to them.

Ron Farr has been of great assistance to me throughout this project but particularly at the beginning. Ron's expertise lies in his knowledge of ships and maritime matters in general. In the early stages of my research I often struggled to understand matters relating to Gus' time as a merchant seaman and salvage expert. Ron was always willing to offer his expertise and never once laughed at my very basic questions. He helped in identifying ships, proof-read the entire book and it was Ron who told me of the existence of the painting of the *Dunraven* which is shown on the back cover. I am indebted to him for his considerable help and advice.

A number of organisations and individuals have provided images or copyright permission to reproduce images or quote from a published work. They are: Aberdeen Art Gallery and Museum; Amgueddfa Cymru-National Museum Wales; Associated Newspapers; Bishop Vesey's School; Neil Clark; Kim J. Gargett; Guildhall Library, City of Lodon Corporation; John Hunt; Imperial War Museum, London; Lloyds of London; Peter Newcombe; Periscope Publishing; Dave Phillips; The Royal Society of Marine Artists; John Sale; Len Sellers; Stephen Snelling; *The Walsall Observer*; Alfie Windsor. Several of those listed have also kindly shared their expertise.

Others who have contributed include: Edward Besley; Mark Chirnside; Shaz and Rob Ellis; Meredith Greiling; Jean Griffiths; Richard Keen; Jan Keohane; Ant Moulton; Peter Newcombe; Anthony Porter; Ian Pyke; Mike Smith; SR Print Management; Andrew Watkins. I must also acknowledge the contribution of members of the Great War Forum (**www.1914-18.net**) who have very generously shared their knowledge and expertise on many occasions.

FOREWORD

By David Partridge

For some time now I have had in mind that a book should be written about the life of my uncle, Gus Bonner, because not only was he awarded the Victoria Cross but he also had a most interesting life at sea, both before and after the First World War. He served 'before the mast' on sailing ships and also on merchant ships of all types and sizes, and went on to spend the final decades of his life as a sea salvage officer.

I took this photograph during one of our family holidays. Left to right are Dolly Bonner (Gus' sister), Kitty Partridge (Gus' sister and my mother), my brother Thomas Michael Partridge, Cissy Bonner (Gus' wife), Thomas Herbert Partridge (Cissy's brother and my father) and Gus. The young man crouching at their feet is Gordon Dunraven Bonner (Gus and Cissy's son).

I had an inspired moment when I asked Mrs Sue Satterthwaite to write the book as I have been greatly impressed with her dedication to the task, the thoroughness of her research and the way in which her writing has brought into the story the details of so many other brave men with whom Gus came into contact. I consider that Sue has produced a most readable book which I hope will be found of interest by all those who love the sea and have a concern for seafarers, as well as those who want to learn more about the life of a man who was awarded the most coveted of medals: the Victoria Cross.

Gus was my mother's elder brother and he also married my father's sister and the Bonners and Partridges were a very close family. All of our holidays: at Easter, in the summer and at Christmas, were always spent together. For eight years from 1931 to 1938 inclusive (when I was aged eleven to eighteen) we spent our summer holidays in the same hotel in North Berwick. During those years, Gus was chief sea salvage officer of the Leith Salvage and Towage Company and there was a clause in his contract with that company that even during the holidays, should there be an emergency, he was obliged to be on the dock at Leith within one hour of a telephone call; North Berwick was the ideal place to holiday in order to comply with this provision. I can recollect two occasions when he was called out to work whilst on holiday during those years. One when I accompanied him to view a ship which had gone aground off Holy Island and another to attend a conference with ship owners in a hotel in Grangemouth. Those years were before the age of television and the evenings in the hotel were often spent with Gus telling stories of his life at sea. He was a great raconteur.

In February 1951 Gus died from lung cancer which may have been caused by his heavy smoking or, from the oil found on ships such as the battleship HMS *Royal Sovereign* which had been lent to Russia in 1944. On her return to this country, *Royal Sovereign* was handed over to Gus (in his capacity as the Executive Officer in the region for the British Iron and Steel Corporation), so that he could arrange her onward journey to the ship-breaking yards at Inverkeithing. After he had inspected the ship he returned home with his body covered in oil which had been left behind by the Russians. His wife believed that this oil may have been the cause of his cancer.

I visited him at his home in Edinburgh during his last illness and I can still visualise him sitting up in bed laughing and cracking jokes though in severe pain for which he was sucking morphine tablets. When I left he said, "Goodbye Bunny", as he stretched forward to shake my hand for the last time. He always called me 'Bunny' for a reason I cannot remember as no one else ever called me by that name. Within a week he had died.

From a very early age, Gus had had a desire to have a life at sea and he so pestered his parents about this that, in desperation, his mother wrote to the captain of the naval training ship HMS *Conway* to request that her son be given a cadetship there. The request was granted and so began the life at sea which Gus had dreamed of. I do hope that the younger generation will read this book and become aware of some of the glorious history of the British Royal and Merchant Navies which are now becoming smaller and smaller. Gus' story will inspire them all and, I hope, urge them too to fulfil their dreams.

I am most grateful to members of Gus' family and particularly his grand-daughter Mrs Penelope Buik and her husband David, and his great-grandson, James Bonner, for providing material about Gus for inclusion in the book.

Gus was the first president of the Aldridge Branch of the Royal British Legion and I myself have the honour of being the current president. It is seems fitting, therefore, that any profits which are made from the sale of this book will be donated to the Poppy Appeal.

PREFACE

In June 2007 Gus Bonner's nephew, David Partridge, invited me to his home to ask whether I would consider writing the biography of his uncle. I had first met Mr Partridge when I interviewed his wife, Madge, for one of my previous books and, as the president of the local branch of the Royal British Legion, his is a familiar face to anyone who attends the Remembrance Day parade in Aldridge. When I arrived at his home, I found the dining table covered with boxes, folders and albums, each containing an amazing amount of original material. I had never seen such a wealth of information concerning the life of any individual, let alone a VC, and I recall that I sat there in stunned silence. Quite what Mr Partridge made of my reaction I do not know but he was, as always, very polite and arranged to deliver everything to my house the following week.

During the next few months I worked my way through the information and soon discovered that the fact that Gus Bonner belonged to a very elite group of men, - those whose courage in the face of the enemy had earned them the Victoria Cross - the award of his VC was just one part of what had been a very interesting career at sea. Here was a man whose bravery, adventures and skill were featured in newspapers from as early as 1906, right up to his obituary in 'The Times' in 1951. As well as being a VC, he had also been a cadet on the naval training ship 'Conway,' been granted his Masters Certificate at the tender age of twenty-two, won the Distinguished Service Cross, been the weekend guest of the King and Queen and captained his own Q-ship. In 1920 he and his family moved to Edinburgh where he had a very successful career as a salvage officer, salvaging what had been the biggest ship in the world and even being flown to Norway at the military rank of major to advise on the salvage of the iconic German battleship 'Tirpitz.' Not bad for the son of a Staffordshire farmer who had been born just about as far from the sea as it is possible to be in England.

Almost six months into the project, I began to realise that although I had amassed a great deal of factual information, I did not feel that I 'knew' Gus Bonner. I had read many of his letters and filed them away in their relevant files but I decided to spend an evening reading them again in order to try and build up a picture of Gus the man; it was only then that I understood my difficulty. As you will see as you read this book, Gus Bonner had a great deal to be proud of, yet his letters only contain the very briefest details of what was happening in his own life; preferring instead to enquire after other people.

Gus was not a man to hog the limelight, in fact he positively tried to avoid it. Two very good examples of this concern the award of his VC and DSC. When the people of Aldridge received the news that 'one of their own' had been awarded the Victoria Cross, they began to make arrangements to welcome their local hero. As is described in detail in chapter six, Gus was very (deliberately?) vague about when he might be coming home and, as rumours spread that Gus was in Walsall, people lined the streets around the railway station to welcome him. It turned out to be a false alarm and it appears that when Gus became aware of the reception which was being planned for him he wrote to give an arrival date of two days after his planned arrival. Even his last minute telegram to his parents was not entirely accurate: he arrived at the family home, Manor Farm, two hours before his wire had said he was due! He didn't escape altogether though, and the local newspaper describes him as looking ill at ease as speaker after speaker sang his praises at a packed public meeting in the village.

Gus was not interested in speaking publicly about the award of his VC but, in 1930, he did agree to write about the encounter between the Q-ship *Pargust* and the German mine-laying U-boat, UC29, the action in which he had won the DSC. His lengthy account is reproduced in full in chapter four but it has a couple of glaring omissions: he does not mention the fact that the collective bravery of the men of the *Pargust* was such that the ship was awarded the Victoria Cross, thereby making naval history, nor does he mention what he actually did during the action or why he was awarded the DSC!

Although both Gus' letters and the newspaper reports of his conduct, show him to be a modest and unassuming man, he was not shy. He could be the life and soul of the party, maintaining his sense of humour, even in difficult times. Several people, including Gordon Campbell VC and Harold Auten VC spoke not just of his bravery on the Q-ship *Dunraven* which earned him his VC but also of his cheery disposition which, they said, raised everyone's spirits during very difficult circumstances. In the foreword of this book, David Partridge recalls that even though Gus was in great pain at the end of his life, he still remained cheerful and shared a joke with his visitors.

A further indication of the kind of man Gus Bonner was, comes from the letters and comments of his friends. He maintained friendships for many years and was clearly a loyal friend with a concern for others. He corresponded with Admiral Sir Lewis Bayly from the end of the Great War until Admiral Bayly's death in 1936; men who once discussed subjects vital to the outcome of the war, now wrote about holidays and their families. Both Gus and his former captain, Gordon Campbell VC, led very busy lives after the war but still made the effort to keep in touch with one another; Rear-Admiral Campbell even came to Aldridge in 1938 to support his friend at the opening of the British Legion Hall of which Gus was president. Theirs was a friendship formed in war, borne of mutual respect, which was to last until the end of their lives. On more than one occasion, both from a public platform and in print, Gordon Campbell described Gus as the bravest man he had ever met; much to Gus' embarrassment no doubt!

I have used many quotes from family letters, official documents, newspaper articles and correspondence between friends in order to try and show the kind of man Gus Bonner was. Although the facts of his life are interesting in themselves, I hope that the addition of a personal and often humorous perspective will add to the enjoyment of the reader.

I cannot end this introduction without offering my thanks to the man who caused Bonner VC to be written: his nephew David Partridge. It was quite clear from the early days of this project that he and I would have a good working relationship. The very first thing he showed me when I went to see him was not any of the important official documents which are reproduced in this book, nor was it one of the many newspaper articles extolling the bravery of his Uncle Gus; it was the very small and badly damaged family holiday snap which has been repaired and reproduced in his foreword. It was evident to me then that the publication of his uncle's biography was to be a labour of love and, as both of us were of the same mind, working with him has been a pleasure. He has allowed me unrestricted access to his family's precious photographs, documents and letters and not only met all expenses concerned with the project but has also said that any profits which we may make from the sale of this book are to be donated to the Royal British Legion Poppy Appeal. I am very grateful to him for providing me with a project which most military historians would give their right arm for, whilst also giving me the freedom to write as I wanted to and being willing to offer advice, assistance and encouragement whenever I needed it.

More than ninety years ago Reverend Tarleton, vicar of Aldridge Parish Church, told a packed public meeting in the village that he felt that the bravery of our local hero was such that he would one day be the subject of a book. It is largely due to the generosity and determination of David Partridge that Gus Bonner's biography has been written. Right at the beginning of this project he said, in an understated way which is so reminiscent of his uncle, that he felt that Gus had had an interesting life which some people might enjoy reading about. I very much hope that you, the reader, will gain as much pleasure from reading this book as I have had in writing it.

Sue Satterthwaite

Chapter 1

THE EARLY YEARS

When Jane Bonner, nee Hellaby, gave birth to her second son on December 29th 1884 in the small hill-top village of Shuttington in Warwickshire, three miles from Tamworth, she and her husband Samuel struggled to decide on a name for him. They had faced no such decision when their first child, Samuel Robinson Bonner, had been born almost two years earlier: it being a long held family tradition, stretching back at least four generations, that the first born Bonner son was given the name of Samuel. Eventually, after more than five weeks deliberation, they decided to do what many modern-day parents do: name their new son after a well-known personality! Having heard of the brave fight of General Gordon and his men at Khartoum, a man for whom she had a great deal of admiration, Jane suggested that their new son should be given his Christian names: Charles George. Yet for some reason which no one seemed to know (including the man himself), Charles George Bonner was always known as Gus.

The tiny church of St Matthew, Shuttington, where Gus was baptised.

Gus' father, Samuel Bonner, the son of Samuel and Mary, had been born in 1855 in Barwell, Leicestershire. As a young man Samuel worked on his father's farm, moving on to gain experience on other farms in the district before eventually moving to Mount Farm, Grendon where he farmed three hundred and sixty-six acres and employed four men and six boys. He married Jane Hellaby, one of seven children of Charles and Katherine Hellaby of Bramcote Hall near Polesworth, Warwickshire on 9th March 1882. The census record of 1861 shows four year old Jane Hellaby at Bramcote Hall where her father farmed eight hundred and fifty-two acres, employing fourteen men and five women. By 1881 Jane had left the family home and was employed as a governess to three sons of a Canadian vicar living near Burton-on-Trent.

The early years of Sam and Jane's married life were spent at Mount Farm where their first child, Samuel, was born; moving to Foremark Farm in Derbyshire at sometime in 1884. On 11th October 1884 the young family moved to Church Farm, Shuttington where Sam Bonner was employed as a farm bailiff. Gus was born at Church Farm just two months later, being baptised at the tiny church of St Matthews, Shuttington on January 25th 1885. Shuttington was a very small village at the time of his birth, with a population of approximately four hundred and having five farms, two shops and a pub. However, Gus would have had no recollection of his birthplace, the family having moved to Aldridge, Staffordshire in August 1885 when he was less than eight months old.

It is believed that the young family came to Aldridge because Jane Bonner had relatives in the area: her sister, Dora Hellaby, having married a prominent local farmer, John Myatt. Aldridge was a much bigger parish than Shuttington with a population of approximately two thousand. Trade directories show that when the Bonner family came to the village, Aldridge had two colliery companies, two brick and tile making firms and no fewer than sixteen farms. There was also a post office, savings bank, grocers, butchers, stationers, four boot and shoe makers and five pubs.

Aldridge High Street. The Bonner family are believed to have lived in one of the cottages on the left of this picture. (Courtesy of the John Sale Collection.)

Sam Bonner worked as farm bailiff to Dr Cooke of the Manor House, the family living in two different houses in the village before taking over Manor Farm in 1894 when Sam Bonner became the tenant farmer. By that time Gus had two sisters; Ursula Catherine (known as Kitty) who was born 25th February 1886 and Mary Elizabeth born 3rd February 1892. Sam and Jane's fifth and final child, Helen Dorothy (known as Dolly), was born 30th April 1894, shortly after the family moved to Manor Farm.

The farm, which was approximately one hundred years old when the Bonners took up residence, had a lovely outlook. On one side was the Manor House, on the other the Parish Church and to the front was the Croft, a large piece of open land which still exists today but is not quite as lovely as it once was. In the hallway of this imposing house, several important documents from the family's history were proudly displayed on the walls, including a draw ticket for the conscripted militia dated 1823, a catalogue of sale dated 1793 and a framed document making Gus' great-grandfather a freeman of the borough of Leicester. The farmhouse had several rooms downstairs which included a drawing room, sitting room and large kitchen. Upstairs there were four bedrooms, with a further three small adjoining rooms in the attic.

Kitty, Sam and Gus. Probably taken in 1890.

Sam and Jane Bonner were hard working middle class people who not only ran a successful farm and raised their five children but also took a great interest in the local community and charitable causes. Gus grew up in a family with a strong work ethic; an example which he and his siblings would follow.

SCHOOLDAYS.

When Gus was eight years old, he and Samuel were enrolled at Bishop Vesey's School Sutton Coldfield, sitting the entrance examination on September 18th 1893. Prior to this time it would appear that Gus and Samuel were taught at home, as were their three sisters.

Bishop Vesey's School is one of the oldest schools in England: being founded in 1527 by the Bishop of Exeter, John Vesey. In 1896 the school prospectus shows that the fees were six pounds and fifteen shillings per year, with a number of extras to be paid for separately. These included seven shillings per term for chemicals, twelve shillings and sixpence for equipment used in the laboratory, three guineas for school meals, and an additional charge for lessons in wood carving, instrumental music, dancing and fencing. The standard curriculum included the following lessons:

Holy Scripture and Religious Knowledge.	Grammar.	Literature.
Reading, Writing and Dictation.	Geography.	History.
Arithmetic and Mensuration.	Bookkeeping.	Shorthand.
Algebra, Geometry and Trigonometry.	Chemistry.	French.
Drawing and Drilling.	Latin.	Greek.
Natural Philosophy.		

The prospectus goes on to describe some of the facilities at the school, including more than ten acres of playing fields, cricket pavilion, laboratory, library and an infirmary.

Bishop Vesey's School, Sutton Coldfield. Gus and his brother Samuel were pupils here from 1893-1898. (Courtesy of Bishop Vesey's School.)

In 1896 Bishop Vesey's School had a total of sixty pupils which included ten boarders; by the time Gus left, pupil numbers had risen to seventy-seven. Gus and Samuel did not board there but, when Samuel left the school in 1898, Sam and Jane took the decision to transfer their youngest son to Coleshill Grammar School where he was enrolled as a boarder The reason for the move is unclear but it is possible that Sam and Jane had decided that a few terms as a boarder would prepare their son for his chosen career: a life at sea. Amongst the many letters which have been kept by the Bonner family one, sent by Gus from Coleshill, is quite amusing. One of the masters had bought a wonderful new contraption called a typewriter and allowed the boys to use it to send a letter home. Gus found it very exciting and although his spelling was probably fine, a letter he sent to his father was somewhat difficult to read because he hadn't quite mastered the skill of hitting one key at a time or of using the 'caps lock' key efficiently! He spent four terms at Coleshill, leaving at the end of the summer term 1899.

HMS CONWAY.

From a very young age, all Gus ever wanted to do was to have a career at sea. Amongst his personal papers are two copies of a magazine called 'The Cadet,' dated 1897. 'The Cadet' was a publication of the school ship HMS *Conway* which trained young men for a career as officers in the Merchant Marine. The magazines are full of stories from boys who had been trained on *Conway* and who were now leading exciting lives at sea; tales of friendly and not so friendly natives on far-flung islands, weird and wonderful animals, birds and sea-creatures, Portuguese pirates and the rescue of the crew of a ship-wreck. It should be noted that not all of these stories had a happy ending, some being positively gruesome but obviously not gruesome enough to deter the son of a Staffordshire farmer who had been born as far away from England's coast as it was possible to be. In 1899, Jane Bonner wrote to *Conway* asking for an application form and by September her youngest son had become Cadet Charles George Bonner.

By the time Cadet Bonner took up residence, HMS *Conway* already had a proud, forty year history. In April 1858 a committee had been formed by the Mercantile Marine Service Association with the aim of establishing a training ship on the Mersey to prepare boys for the role of Merchant Officers. The Admiralty offered the frigate *Conway* for the purpose which was subsequently moored off Rock Ferry near Birkenhead, opening as a training establishment on August 1st 1859. The frigate was replaced after two years and again in 1876 when HMS *Nile* became the third and final floating *Conway*, although HMS *Conway* continued as a shore base until 1974.

The life of a *Conway* cadet was, of necessity, not an easy one because the young men who trained in her were not embarking on an easy career. They might eventually have responsibility for not only a ship and its cargo, but also the lives of both the men under their command and any passengers which their ship might be carrying. In his book '*HMS Conway 1859-1974*,' author Alfie Windsor wrote of the training which a cadet would receive:

> "It was always physically and mentally testing, but the end result was
> invariably the same. Seventeen year old men ready to go to sea and do their duty.
> Life at sea, then and now, was not for the faint-hearted. It was a tough,
> difficult and demanding life. It required men with a steady heart, a firm
> nerve and a ready hand."

The ship's motto was taken from Corinthians 1:13 'Quit Ye Like Men And Be Strong.' Gus and his fellow cadets joined the *Conway* as boys but left as men.

HMS 'Conway.'
(Courtesy of HMS 'Conway' 1859-1974 by Alfie Windsor.)

THE SHIP.

Gus was aged fourteen years and eight months when he became a *Conway* cadet, Sam and Jane paying fifty-two pounds ten shillings a year in fees, six pounds ten shillings for the provision and laundering of his clothes, and four pounds for 'extras.' On a September day in 1899 he made what would soon become a very familiar trip by rowing boat, out to the ship which was to be home to him and approximately one hundred and seventy other boys for the next two years. He was given a black sea-chest which had his name painted on it and, on opening the lid, he found a shallow removable wooden tray for holding small items. The space under the tray was for storing clothing: an all in one wardrobe and chest of drawers! This chest would be his only little bit of private space and no cadet ever looked inside another's sea-chest without permission. Although each was supplied with a padlock, they were rarely used: theft being viewed as the most heinous of crimes.

The first skill which Gus and his fellow new cadets (nicknamed the New Chums) had to master was how to sling a hammock; it was wise to pay close attention and learn quickly if they wanted to sleep that night! Over the coming days they had to familiarise themselves with what was, in effect, a floating multi-storey building. Several cadets have likened the *Conway* to Nelson's flagship *Victory* which is now in dry dock at Portsmouth as a tourist attraction.

The 'front door' of HMS 'Conway'. Cadet Bonner arrived here in September 1899.
(Courtesy of HMS 'Conway' 1859-1974 by Alfie Windsor.)

In order to understand what the ship was like it might be helpful to try and imagine being a visitor taking a guided tour. Cadets, staff and visitors all docked alongside a small platform fixed to the side of the ship and then made their way up a short flight of steps to the 'front door' of the *Conway*; beyond it lay the lower deck. This deck had accommodation space for senior cadet captains (the equivalent of senior prefects in a 'normal' school) who had the luxury of lockers in which to store their belongings and the use of the old gunroom for privacy and relaxation. The lower deck also contained the sick bay with its seven beds and resident nurse, several small cabins for members of staff, two classrooms where seamanship classes were held and the main ablutions area of the ship. Water had to be brought in by boat to supply the sixty-five hand basins and fourteen baths, although it would appear that the water pressure was not up to modern standards, with cadets describing:

> "The near normal ritual of having to suck water from the taps before
> a miserable flow might give you a basin full."

Quite what modern-day psychologists would make of another area of the lower deck can only be guessed at, it being reserved for the boys who were in the habit of wetting their hammocks. In a bid to cure them, their hammocks were strung close to the night-heads: four urinals and one lavatory which were the only ones which could be used at night. Cadets who were responsible for the night watch were required to wake these boys - affectionately referred to as piss-quicks or water lilies - every two or three hours in order for them to use the urinals. Failure to wake the water-lilies would result in punishment for the night watchman should any 'accidents' have occurred.

A small area of the lower deck had display boards recording the achievements of old *Conways*, one of the most notable in Gus' day being Captain Matthew Webb, the first man to swim the Channel from England to France. Over the years *Conway* was to have many famous old boys including admirals, commodores, generals, sportsmen, politicians and even a Poet Laureate in John Masefield, who was never able to have the life at sea which he had trained for because of chronic sea-sickness. Young Cadet Bonner could scarce have imagined that one day his name would be displayed on that board as one of four *Conway* cadets to win the Victoria Cross.

A row of sea-chests on the Orlop deck.
(Courtesy of HMS 'Conway' 1859-1974 by Alfie Windsor.)

The deck immediately below the lower deck was called the Orlop Deck, this was to be where Gus and his fellow cadets were to spend much of their time. One area of the deck had long tables and benches where boys could sit and, at night, they would sling their hammocks along the length of the ship, near to their sea-chests; each cadet's hammock being approximately two and a half feet off the ground and two feet away from his nearest neighbour. During the day hammocks were stored in two large bins and cadets sat on the benches or made use of their sea-chests; sitting on top of them or opening the lid to use it as a recliner.

Although the Orlop deck was quite open during the daytime, not all boys could pass along it freely. As a new cadet Gus was only allowed on the part of the deck where his fellow intake had their sea-chests. If he wanted to pass into an area of the deck where more senior cadets resided, he would have had to ask their permission, even if he had to go there as part of his cleaning duties. By his second term he would have moved slightly further along the deck and new cadets would then have to ask his approval to progress along the deck, although Gus still had to ask to be allowed to enter the domain of more senior boys. Only in his final months on board would he have been allowed to walk the entire deck without asking anyone for permission. New cadets were allowed two weeks grace to accustom themselves to life on board, after which they were expected to fit in.

Beneath the Orlop Deck was the Hold, a large open space which had once housed the ship's engines but was now a makeshift gymnasium/recreation area, complete with boxing ring. The cadets' reading room, seating fifteen, was located on the port side and a few cadets called the 'Hold Party' slept down here in the bowels of the ship. The only remaining area below the Hold was the bilge: a dark and very low space frequented only by those responsible for its upkeep, the occasional illicit smoker, and rats.

Had one proceeded to climb up rather than down when entering the ship, the first deck to be reached from the lower deck was the main deck where there were cabins for various members of staff, a kitchen and a large open area which had three purposes: it was the mess deck where the cadets ate and spent recreation time, a dormitory at night and, with the help of hinged wooden screens, provided four separate classrooms during the daytime. Also on this deck were glass-fronted cabinets holding trophies awarded for sporting achievement, and an area of 'holy ground,' consecrated by the Bishop.

The top or upper deck of the ship was dominated by the mighty masts with their mass of rigging. At the front end was the forecastle, a raised area with a deck reached by a short ladder, which could be used by any boy and was a favourite place to 'lounge.' At the other end lay the poop deck with the positively palatial captain's quarters underneath, comprising a sitting room, morning room, dining room and two bedrooms. How the boys sleeping below in bunks two feet apart would have marvelled at the way their captain lived!

A CADET'S LIFE.

For Gus and his fellow cadets the day began with Reveille at 6.00 after which they washed, dressed, and cleaned part of the ship: each boy being responsible for the cleanliness of a specific area of the vessel. Breakfast at 7.45 consisted of bread, jam or marmalade, oatmeal or porridge and coffee. Prayers were said both before and after breakfast and then lessons followed until noon. The ship's routine was deliberately arranged to closely match what would be experienced when the cadets left to begin their careers at sea. The boys were divided into two groups and named Port and Starboard Watch. In the morning one watch would attend practical seamanship classes and the other academic lessons, swapping round in the afternoon. Seamanship classes were held on deck, aloft, or in one of the ship's small boats, while academic lessons were taught on the main deck. Generally speaking the cadets took their seamanship classes very seriously but tended to see the academic part of the curriculum as something of little relevance. Uniformed staff were afforded a great deal more respect than those who wore the gowns of an academic. The certificate awarded to Gus at the end of his training shows the skills which he acquired during his time as a *Conway* cadet.

Lunch was the main meal of the day and consisted of a main course such as corned beef or roast pork and potatoes, followed by a sweet such as jam tart or fresh fruit tart; tea and coffee being supplied as required. Afternoon lessons began at 14.00, after which the cadets cleaned the decks before having tea, bread, butter and jam at 19.10. Various activities took place during the evening, including homework, letter-writing boxing, debating, fencing, reading, writing, playing games, using the facilities of the gymnasium, lounging on either sea-chest or deck or climbing the mast to enjoy the view as well as the relative peace and quiet. Cadets recall a constant background noise all over the ship as boys called out to one another. A favourite cry was, 'sodduck for spread' which meant that a cadet had some bread which he wanted to swap for a spread of jam. In order for announcements to be made or orders given, a 'still' would

Climbing the mast was a popular pastime for the 'Conway' cadets. (Courtesy of HMS 'Conway' 1859-1974 by Alfie Windsor.)

be sounded on the bugle and everyone was expected to keep quiet and listen. Whether they actually heard anything was another matter: cadets recalling that the announcements were incomprehensible, rather like those on a railway station. No wonder the boys liked to climb the mast!

Once a week there was a concert or lecture, with the captain's wife always ready to offer a recitation or lead the boys in the singing of popular songs. Old *Conways* were encouraged to return to the ship to inspire the boys with their stories of a life at sea, a life which the cadets could experience for themselves within a few weeks of leaving the ship. At the end of the evening came prayers, tea and biscuits, the playing of the Last Post and lights out at 21.00.

Wednesday, Saturday and Sunday saw slightly different timetables. Wednesday and Saturday afternoons were usually reserved for sport, with the boys taking to the boats to visit either the public baths or the ship's playing fields which were situated in Birkenhead. In winter they played football and in the summer cricket, although the situation and condition of the field was not conducive to either: the grass being coarse and lumpy with the river on one side and a brook on the other. As a further hindrance to sporting excellence it was on a slope! Rowing and sailing were year-round activities. Saturday and Sunday mornings were taken up with 'sweeps' i.e. cadets thoroughly cleaning whichever part of the ship they had responsibility for in preparation for Captain Miller's inspection after church.

Archibald T Miller, *Conway's* fourth captain who had joined the ship in 1881, was well respected by the cadets who had nick-named him 'Lippy' because of his prominent lower lip which seemed to thrust out even more when he was annoyed. When he joined *Conway* Captain Miller found the ship in a somewhat lax state and set about getting her in working order. He had decking installed in the Hold to create the

'Conway's' captain, Archibald (Lippy) Miller, with some of the ship's cadets.
(Courtesy of HMS 'Conway' 1859-1974 by Alfie Windsor.)

gymnasium and lecture hall, erected a thirty foot high training mast to teach rigging and installed electric lights. Captain Miller was also responsible for standardising the ships uniform, insisting that all cadets were to purchase their uniform from the Liverpool Sailors Home; previously it could be bought from any source from a list of specifications. The uniform included a blue Glengarry style cap which was only ever worn on the ship, never when they were in boats or ashore. It had white mottling at the edges, a dark blue pompom and long black silk ribbons which were quickly removed as part of a new recruit's initiation. Gus and his fellow cadets soon learnt how to sew - if they could not do so already - as they were responsible for mending their own clothes.

Cadets had two months holiday a year. Gus was at home at Manor Farm at the time of the 1901 census and described as being sixteen years old and a sailor (sea-cadet). His older brother Samuel was an apprentice engineer, Kitty was away at boarding school in Bristol and Mary and Dolly were being taught by a governess.

Everything and everyone travelled to and from *Conway* by boats which were operated by the boys themselves. If the sea was rough or the wind too strong, boats would not venture out, sometimes for days at a time. This brought mixed blessings: deliveries of food and water could be interrupted but, on the plus side, the teachers who lived ashore could not get to the ship to conduct lessons! In modern times the news that one hundred and seventy boys were trapped on a ship for days on end with little food or water would make national headlines. In 1899 it was just seen as a part, if an unwelcome one, of the boys training for the kind of conditions which they might experience in their chosen career. Something else which would be unacceptable in the 21st century, was the disposal of rubbish and effluent. The ship was kept clean and was always free from litter: rubbish being placed in 'yak tubs' around the ship and then simply thrown overboard! Effluent made its way into the Mersey via a large square pipe on the outside of the ship, being dispersed by the tidal stream.

Gus was allowed two baths a week if he wanted them, although from all accounts the experience would not have been a pleasant one, with younger cadets being second or third in line to use the bath water which,

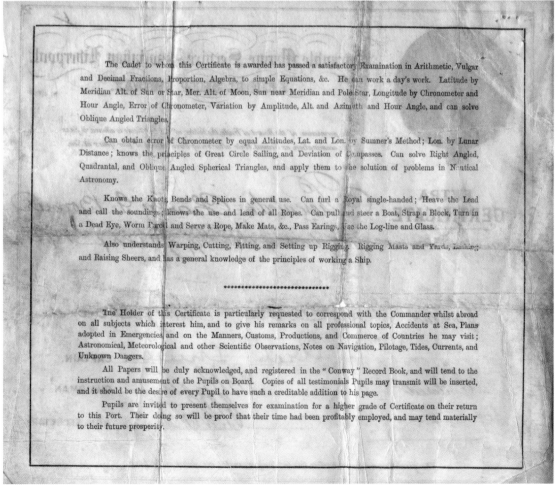

This certificate was presented to Gus when he left 'Conway'. His training had provided a thorough grounding for what was to be a successful and eventful life at sea.

The reverse of Gus' conduct certificate showing some of the skills he had learnt during his cadetship.

after other occupants, was both luke warm and dirty. It was said that junior cadets often came out dirtier than they went in and then they had the unenviable task of scrubbing the grime off the bath!

Cadet Bonner's reports were divided into two categories. His naval report, which was an assessment of the practical aspects of his training, consistently rated his ability as good, his conduct as good or very good and his application as satisfactory or very good. Comments on the academic aspect of his training ranged from fair to very good.

Gus had few mentions in 'The Cadet' magazine during his two years on Conway. He did not win any academic or technical prizes, nor is their any mention of him in the sports teams, although he did row in the ship's twelve-oared cutters and was selected to compete in the annual race against another training ship. For some reason, possibly illness or injury, he did not take part in the actual event. But, one item in 'The Cadet' which is of particular interest, is one which shows that, on the 6th June 1900, Gus was confirmed into the Church of England by the Bishop of Liverpool, Francis Chavasse. Bishop Chavasse's son Noel, who was about the same age as Gus, would go on to become one of the most iconic men of the Great War, being awarded the Military Cross as well as the Victoria Cross and Bar for his quite extraordinary bravery.

Conway would continue as a cadet training ship for many years but in 1953, whilst travelling through the Menai Straits bound for a re-fit at Birkenhead, a sudden strong tide drove her ashore. Thousands of well-wishers who had been waiting to cheer her on her way through the Straits were horrified to find themselves as witnesses to the end of this great ship. Many thousands more came to see the wreck which remained on the Menai for three years until she eventually caught fire.

In July 1901 Gus and two of his fellow cadets left Conway to begin their apprenticeship on the Aberdeen based ship, Invermark. Although he would eventually become famous because of the action in 1917 which was to earn him a VC, it would not be the first occasion on which his name appeared in national newspapers, or the first time he almost lost his life. The years between the start of his apprenticeship and the award of his VC were to see him involved in adventures every bit as exciting as the ones which he had read about in 'The Cadet' or heard about on Conway.

Chapter 2

THE CALL OF THE SEA

On 12th July 1901, an apprenticeship indenture in the name of Charles George Bonner was registered at the port of Aberdeen on the Scottish east coast. The indenture, which was a legally binding document, was signed by seven signatories including two of Gus' uncles and his father, Samuel Bonner, who stood surety of £31:10s for his son.

This apprenticeship indenture shows that Gus received a total of £27 for the three years in which he was apprenticed to George Milne.

Gus was apprenticed to George Milne and Company and it was Mr Milne himself who signed Gus' indenture; promising to teach him the business of a seaman and to provide him with the following during the period of his apprenticeship:

> "Sufficient meat, drink, lodging, medicine and medical and surgical assistance."

In addition, George Milne agreed to pay Gus £5 for the first year of his apprenticeship, £9 for the second and £13 for the third.

13

For his part, Gus had to promise (amongst other things) to faithfully serve his master, not embezzle or waste his goods, not to play unlawful games and not to frequent taverns or alehouses unless on the company's business!

Gus was appointed to the 1,436 ton, three-masted steel barque (small sailing ship) *Invermark* which had been built in 1890 by Russell and Co. of Glasgow. His first voyage was to New York via Le Havre and during his apprenticeship he journeyed to Antwerp, Vancouver, Rangoon, St Helena, Peru and Australia.

During his third year on the *Invermark*, Gus was provided with two references. One was signed by George Milne and reads:

> We hereby certify that App Charles Geo. Bonner has served on our
> barque *Invermark* up to this date and in foreign ports a period of two
> years six months and thirteen days since the register of his indenture
> at Aberdeen on the 12th July 1901.

The other reference came from the Master of the *Invermark*, Alfred Bolderston, who wrote:

> Antwerp. April 11th 1904. Barque *Invermark* of Aberdeen. This is to
> certify that Chas G Bonner has served as an apprentice on board the
> above vessel (under my command) from July 1901 until this date.
> During this time I have always found him diligent and attentive
> to his duties and vouch for his good conduct and sobriety.

The barque 'Invermark' on which Gus served a three year apprenticeship.
(Courtesy of Aberdeen Art Gallery and Museums Collection.)

When Alfred Bolderston died several years later, the following article appeared in one of the journals of the mercantile marine:

> Mr C.G. Bonner, Second Officer of the *Muncaster Castle*, New York
> writes- "I have recently been informed of the sad death of one of our
> late members, Captain R.(sic) E. Bolderston. The news of his death
> both shocked and grieved me, I having had the good fortune to serve
> my apprenticeship under his command, 1901-1904. We boys used to
> look upon him as a very hard and severe man. I think we have all
> realised however since, what a fine type of Shipmaster he really
> was, exacting the strictest obedience and enforcing sufficient
> discipline to make his ship comfortable for everyone. He is a great
> loss to the Mercantile Marine."

ALMOST SHIPWRECKED.

In the summer of 1904, Gus left *Invermark* to begin a ten year career as a merchant seaman, during which time he would visit every maritime country in the world apart from New Zealand. Two years later in 1906 came the first of several newspaper articles concerning some of his voyages and adventures.

A Brisbane newspaper reported that the barque *Ashmore* on which Gus was serving as first mate, had had an 'eventful voyage' which had lasted one hundred and eleven days, beginning in Liverpool where they loaded cargo and then on to Glasgow before setting sail for Australia. The journalist who wrote the article described the *Ashmore* as:

> "An excellent example of naval architecture. She is a fine vessel of
> 1099 tons, having clipper bows and exceedingly graceful lines"

He said that he mourned the loss of such beautiful sailing ships from Australia's harbours, describing them as 'white-winged flyers.' His report continues:

> "The vessel is owned by Messrs' John Stewart and Co. London, and
> is under the command of Captain H. Fooks who has been trading to
> and from Australia for over 16 years. Captain Fooks is accompanied
> by Mrs Fooks. The *Ashmore* carries a crew of 21 all told, including
> five apprentices. Mr C.G. Bonner is first officer."

Captain Fooks reported that the ship had left Glasgow on July 1st and experienced fine sailing weather all the way down to the Equator which was crossed on August 5th. Favourable winds saw the *Ashmore* pass the Cape of Good Hope twenty-four days later but then a series of gales began to cause serious difficulties. The weather around the Cape could change suddenly and very dramatically: a calm sea and a glorious sunrise quickly becoming a violent storm of wind, rain, hail or even snow. Captain Fooks said:

> "On September 13th, while the vessel was bowling along under full
> canvas a terrific gale came up from the S.W. All hands were at
> once put on to shorten the sail, but under the circumstances this was
> a dangerous occupation, for the deck was awash with water almost
> continually. While the hands were endeavouring to take in the foresail
> and the main topsail, a huge sea was shipped with such force that it

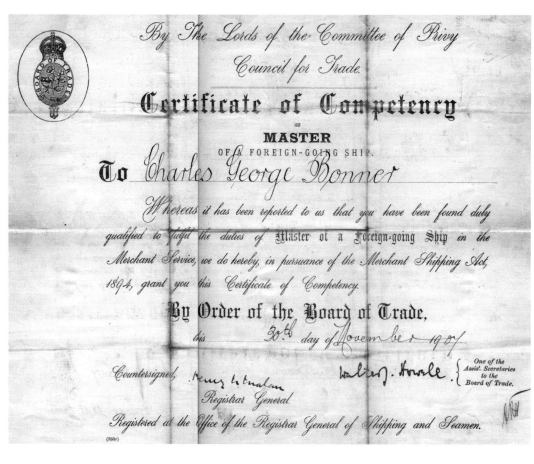

By The Lords of the Committee of Privy
Council for Trade.

Certificate of Competency

as

MASTER

OF A FOREIGN-GOING SHIP.

To Charles George Bonner

Whereas it has been reported to us that you have been found duly qualified to fulfil the duties of Master of a Foreign-going Ship in the Merchant Service, we do hereby, in pursuance of the Merchant Shipping Act, 1894, grant you this Certificate of Competency.

By Order of the Board of Trade,

this 30th day of November 1907

Countersigned, Henry L Grahan
Registrar General.

Walter J Howell { One of the Assis'. Secretaries to the Board of Trade.

Registered at the Office of the Registrar General of Shipping and Seamen.

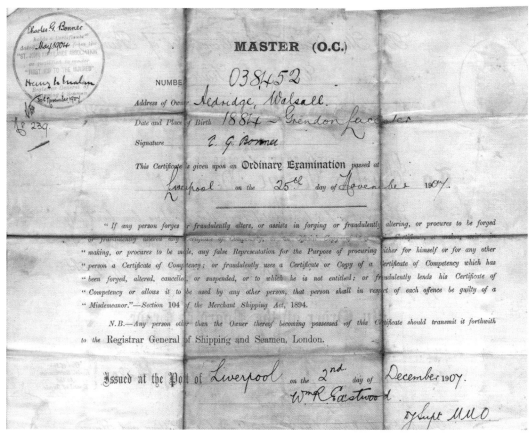

MASTER (O.C.)

NUMBER 038452

Address of Owner Aldridge, Walsall.

Date and Place of Birth 1884 ~ Grendon, Leicester

Signature C. G. Bonner

This Certificate is given upon an **Ordinary Examination** passed at

Liverpool on the 25th day of November 1907.

"If any person forges or fraudulently alters, or assists in forging or fraudulently altering, or procures to be forged or fraudulently altered any Certificate of Competency, or any official copy of any Certificate of Competency; or makes, or assists in "making, or procures to be made, any false Representation for the Purpose of procuring either for himself or for any other "person a Certificate of Competency; or fraudulently uses a Certificate or Copy of a Certificate of Competency which has "been forged, altered, cancelled, or suspended, or to which he is not entitled; or fraudulently lends his Certificate of "Competency or allows it to be used by any other person, that person shall in respect of each offence be guilty of a "Misdemeanor."—Section 104 of the Merchant Shipping Act, 1894.

N.B.—Any person other than the Owner thereof becoming possessed of this Certificate should transmit it forthwith to the Registrar General of Shipping and Seamen, London.

Issued at the Port of Liverpool on the 2nd day of December 1907.

Wm R Eastwood

Supt MMO

Gus was granted his Master's Certificate at the age of 22.

dashed the men against the bulwarks, and disabled the majority of
them. Thus incapacitated, the crew were unable to continue taking
in sail, the result being that the foresail and the main topsail were
blown to ribbons."

One of the crew had been so badly injured that it was believed that he was dead but the Captain's wife,
who acted as nurse to the injured men, managed not just to save his life but also enabled him to return to
work. In the final year of his apprenticeship Gus had passed the St. Johns First Aid examination and so
would have been able to help Mrs Fooks to attend the injured.

As well as having her sails torn to ribbons, much of the *Ashmore* was badly damaged. The after part of the
deck was smashed, the galley (the ships kitchen) had been swept of everything when a wave broke the door
off its hinges, the apprentice quarters had also been completely cleared out, the officer's quarters were
knee deep in water and one of the lifeboats destroyed. At one point during the thirty-six hour
bombardment, the ship broached to, only skilful management enabling her to be righted from a very
dangerous position. Natives from a nearby island attempted to get food out to the ship but the sea proved
to be too rough. However, fine weather eventually returned and the *Ashmore*, her crew and 1600 tons of
cargo arrived safely at their destination.

Gus left the *Ashmore* in October 1907 having served on her for fifteen months. A month later, at the age
of twenty-two, he was awarded his Master's Certificate: a certificate of competency which proved him able
and qualified to fulfil the duties of a master of a foreign-going ship. The document states that he had passed
an 'Ordinary Examination' at Liverpool on November 25th; his certificate being issued at Liverpool on
December 2nd.

JUST DOING HIS JOB.

Gus' nephew recalls quite clearly the story of another of his uncle's adventures as a young merchant
seaman. The vessel is believed to have been the steamer *Guatemala*. Gus said:

"I was the first mate on a small British steamer trading along the
coast of Chile and one of our tasks was to call at some ports along
the coast and pick up lunatics to transport them to the central
asylum at Santiago. We called at one small port and I got off the ship
to go to the compound in which the lunatics were held. My job was
that of escort and to ensure that they boarded the ship and were safely
ensconced in their quarters. A half dozen or so were dealt with but
there was also, in the compound, a man dressed in morning suit with
a top hat and a cravat around his neck secured by a diamond pin. I
went up to him and said, 'Sir I have instructions to escort you to the
ship so that you can travel to Santiago. Come with me this way please.'
The man did not move or say anything so I repeated my speech to him.
Again he remained looking ahead and neither moving or speaking. My
instructions were to get the lunatics on board and, as the man was
sitting in the compound where the lunatics were contained, I said to
him, 'If you will not do as I have requested politely, I must take the
necessary steps to get you on the ship.' And so I got him by the scruff
of the neck and the seat of his pants, and more or less frog-marched
him aboard the ship and took him to his allotted quarters. I then went

to the galley for some refreshment after my efforts but I was not there long before a call came for me to go and see the Captain straightaway. When I got to the Captain's cabin, I saw that seated at the table with him, enjoying a whisky, was the top-hatted gentlemen. 'Bonner, said the Captain, I believe that you may already have met Senor Gonzalez. He is the Home Secretary of Chile. He has come to see how the lunatics are treated during transportation to their new home!"

A FLOATING JUNGLE.

In December 1910, came another report of Gus' adventures at sea, this time from the 'Boston Herald.' The heading for the article was:

"FLOATING JUNGLE REACHES PORT. Elephant, Pythons, Red-Faced Apes and Salamanders on Muncaster Castle. People saved from suicide. Steamship rescued twenty-one from despair on wreck then put torch to hulk."

The story of the voyage of the steamship Muncaster Castle, which was carrying what was described as 'oriental merchandise,' is every bit as bizarre as the headline. A variety of animals, birds and fish were on board. The journalist wrote:

"There was a baby elephant that had the run of the ship gamboling about the deck with all the clumsiness of an overgrown puppy. There were five Siamese red-faced apes who looked as though they had stolen the rouge pot from a make-up box and painted crimson blushes on their hairy cheeks."

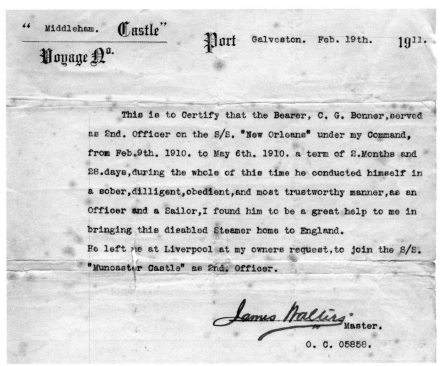

One of the many favourable references which Gus received during his career as a merchant seaman.

The article also describes several unusual fish, seven Victoria Cross pigeons, six orang-utans, a Malay bear, a rare Siamese cat, a Celebes monkey, eight salamanders from Japan, two Chinese snakes (one of whom bit the captain) and a number of pigs.

Gus during a period of leave in April 1912. He and his mother, Jane, and sisters Mary and Dolly are in the garden of Manor Farm.

The description of the pythons and their diet is too gruesome to reproduce verbatim, suffice to say that there were four pythons on board, three of whom succumbed to the cold weather whilst the remaining one laid a hundred eggs in one day and lived on a diet of live animals. The orang-utan ate at the table in the saloon with the captain. The sight of such weird and wonderful creatures on board a merchant vessel was too much for one of the crew who decided that he must give up alcohol. It would appear that he had seen such creatures in the past and vowed that if he ever set eyes on them again he would, as he put it, 'sign the pledge.' Another sailor decided that more drastic action was needed. The article continues:

> "One of the Chinese members of the crew went into the menagerie
> Hold whilst the ship was in the straits of Malacca. Rushing on deck he
> looked over the high sides of the steamer at the water, filled with the
> curved fins of hundreds of sharks and deciding that he would take a
> chance with the sharks rather than stay on such a devil-ship, seized a
> bench and sprang into the sea. He was seen by a quartermaster, and
> Second Officer C.G. Bonner ordered a boat put overboard and the man
> was brought back to the steamer. Now the man is considered a hoodoo."

The '*New York Times*' also reported on the voyage, describing how a spate of bad weather had caused the ship to roll, during which time a crate containing salamanders and crocodiles was broken open. The crocodiles and some of the salamanders were recaptured and it was presumed that the remainder had been washed overboard. However, later in the evening when the crew lit the fire in their quarters, the salamanders were drawn to its warmth, causing the crew to refuse to sleep there! The bad weather had also resulted in the bear's cage being broken open and no sooner had Gus and the rest of the long-suffering crew managed to get the reptiles back in their containers, than they were faced with a Malay bear who had decided to climb the mast to avoid capture.

The voyage of the *Muncaster Castle* had been eventful in other ways. For three weeks during their crossing from Gibraltar, the ship had been continuously battered by gales and heavy seas, suffering some structural damage. Before leaving eastern waters they had come across a dismasted vessel which had been drifting for seventeen days in unbearable heat and was now more than a thousand miles off course. In his report, Captain Watson of the *Muncaster Castle* said:

> "As she came near us we saw a sight seldom given to sailors to see
> and one which chilled our hearts. On board the vessel was a score of
> human beings, all insane and some lying around as though dead. We
> read on the craft the name Futeluted Mubarik."

Captain Watson asked Gus and Lieutenant Donohue, his chief officer, to board the ship along with some of the Chinese crew. They found both the ship and its crew and passengers in a bad way: the ship having four feet of water in its Hold and the people having had no food and water for five days. Those who were able to speak told Gus and Lieutenant Donohue that six vessels had passed by but none had seen their signals of distress and had the *Muncaster Castle* done the same, they had decided that they would take their own lives. The ship had been carrying passengers from Ceylon to Addu Attol (sic) and was within sight of their destination when they had been caught in a monsoon.

Twenty men in a weak and confused state were taken off the ailing ship and the decision made that her decks should be saturated in oil and set alight in order to prevent her becoming a hazard to shipping. As they took their final look around, one of the crew spotted a young girl huddled in the corner. She was in such a state of shock that she could not walk and had to be carried to safety, after which the ship was torched: being ablaze from stem to stern in less than five minutes.

CHRISTMAS 1913.

Christmas 1913 found Gus in reflective mood. A letter addressed to his parents and post-marked Christmas Eve, shows that he was in Liverpool and about to put to sea in the Johnson Line's 3,158 ton cargo liner *Barnesmore*. It is difficult to know what prompted him to send such a letter. Perhaps it was the time of year and thoughts of Christmas back home in Aldridge, or it could be that he was concerned for the health of his parents. I well recall that the first time I read the letter it struck me that had Gus Bonner's life been a work of fiction rather than one of well documented fact, then the reader might find the letter quite unbelievable. The lines which stand out are:

> "I shall soon be 29 now and I hope for the rest of my life shall give you no
> more trouble and anxiety, as I have done in past years. I only hope that you
> live long enough for me to repay you a little for all your kindness and
> forbearance to me. What a selfish pig I have been."

Whether Sam and Jane would have agreed with Gus' assessment of his behaviour is not known but his days of causing them anxiety were far from over. As for his wish that his parents would live long enough to enable him to repay them for their kindness and forbearance, perhaps the award of the Victoria Cross in

1917 would go some way to relieving the guilt which he clearly felt and to helping him realise that he was not such a 'selfish pig' after all.

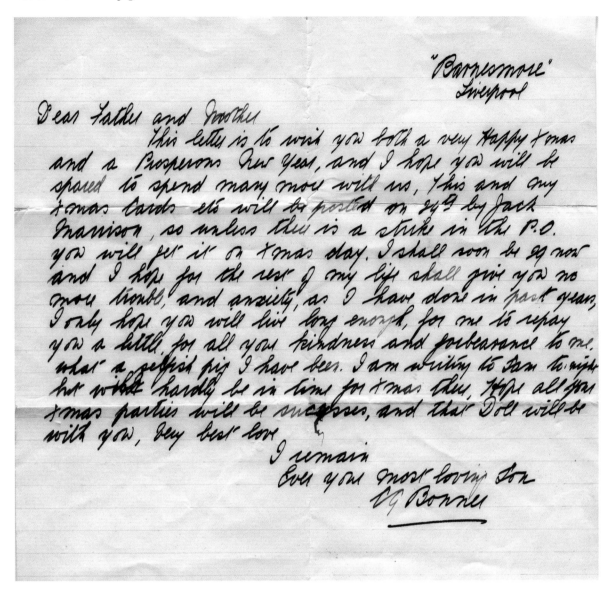

Gus' letter to his parents, posted on Christmas Eve 1913,
in which he describes himself as a 'selfish pig'.

INCEMORE.

Two months before the Great War began, another ship on which Gus had been serving as First Mate since the beginning of April, found itself making front page headlines on both sides of the Atlantic. The ship was the Liverpool-based steamer *Incemore*, part of the Johnson Line, which had been travelling from the Black Sea to Antwerp when she was in collision with the German liner, *Kaiser Wilhelm II*. 'The Times' reported that the *Incemore* had been blowing a warning signal to the liner but suddenly, out of a thick fog, the liner loomed up on her port side and hit her. *The Kaiser Wilhelm* was holed beneath the waterline and, although her captain immediately gave orders to seal the compartments and lower the lifeboats, his order was quickly rescinded when he realised that the damage was confined to one compartment. The liner and its one thousand passengers returned to Southampton for repairs. The *Incemore* did not fare so well: suffering serious damage to her bow and anchor. It must have been a terrifying experience for Gus and the rest of the crew to see this huge liner of more than 20,000 tons suddenly appear towering above their 3,060 ton vessel but, thankfully, no one was injured.

It would appear that the *Incemore* managed to continue her journey but then spent two months in Antwerp, presumably undergoing repairs. During the time they were there the assassination of Archduke Ferdinand, heir to the Austro-Hungarian throne, proved to be the spark which, after decades of tension, ignited a series of events which led to the Great War. Since the Treaty of London in 1839, the neutrality of Belgium had been accepted by all European nations and so when German troops entered Belgium, Britain declared war on Germany.

Records show that the *Incemore* left Antwerp on August 18th, arriving in Cardiff four days later. Interestingly the records of Lloyds show that Gus left the ship on the 17th: the day before she left Antwerp, and the next time that his whereabouts can be confirmed with any certainty is on September 8th when he joined the Royal Naval Volunteer Reserve at the Crystal Palace, London. At the end of the war and in the years which followed, many newspapers published the story of how Gus won his VC. Such reports often included biographical details and all refer to him as being in Antwerp when war broke out and only managing to get back to England because of his Master's Certificate, although the manner of his 'escape' is not given.

VOLUNTEERING.

Records held by the Fleet Air Arm Museum show that Gus enrolled in the London Division of the RNVR on September 8th 1914. This would fit in with the family's recollection that he attended a meeting with First Lord of the Admiralty, Winston Churchill, at the Crystal Palace during which Churchill asked all those who possessed a Master's Certificate to step forward, their details being duly noted. The papers which Gus signed at the time record his trade as 2nd Officer, Merchant Service, Johnson Line, Liverpool, noting that he held a Master's Certificate and that he had fifteen years experience in the merchant service. Other interesting information on the forms show that he was 5ft 9ins tall with a forty inch chest, brown hair, hazel eyes and a tattoo on his right arm. He banked at Barclays Bank in Walsall, was a member of the Church of England and could swim!

The RNVR had been set up in early years of the 20th century as a volunteer reserve of men from all walks of life who were prepared to serve their country if they were ever needed, numbering amongst its ranks those who enjoyed sailing as a hobby and others who simply had a love of the sea. Given Gus' vast experience he would perhaps have been expected to join the Royal Naval Reserve, a similar organisation to the RNVR but one which was made up of merchant seamen and fishermen i.e. those who had training and/or experience of a life at sea. His reasons for choosing to join the RNVR are made quite clear by a man whom he served under during his training at the Crystal Palace. Arthur Egerton Watts wrote that the fact that Gus had joined the RNVR was a remarkable thing considering the fact that he was a Master Mariner. He said that Gus had a feeling that he would not be needed to run a ship during the war and had therefore decided to enlist as an ordinary seaman. His feelings were correct: the Navy had far more volunteers than it needed and Gus' decision to join the RNVR very nearly resulted in him becoming, to all intents and purposes, a soldier. At the Crystal Palace men were formed into battalions of the Royal Naval Division, keeping naval ranks and terminology but undergoing training which prepared them for the life of a soldier. For many such men the only time they were at sea during the Great War was when they were being transported to fight on land. Arthur Watts went on to serve with the Royal Naval Division at Gallipoli but by that time he and Gus had parted company. He wrote:

"They found out he was a fully-qualified man and took him away from me and they commissioned him as a Sub-Lieutenant RNR. Bonner was a nice chap. I liked him."

The seniority date for Gus' commission was 23rd December 1914.

Gus was not the only member of the Bonner family who was to serve his country during the Great War. His older brother Samuel, who had emigrated to Canada, was in a reserved occupation and did not see active service. Samuel would spend the rest of his life in Canada, returning to England just once. He married a Yorkshire girl, Annie Maude Lees, in Vancouver on 3rd October 1910 and by 23rd August 1911 Gus had become an uncle for the first time: Catherine Lees Bonner being the first of three daughters born to Samuel and Annie. However, two of Gus' sisters, Mary and Dolly, did serve as nurses in the Great War. Dolly was honoured by the French for her work as a Voluntary Aid Detachment nurse in Serbia and Salonika, whilst Mary worked at a hospital in Great Yarmouth before joining her sister in Salonika. Fortunately, the Bonner family were not only great letter writers but also great hoarders: the weekly letters which Jane Bonner wrote to her daughters while they were away from home providing an invaluable source of factual, interesting and personal information for this book. The letters begin in 1915 when Dolly went overseas and end in 1919 when Sam and Jane's children came home to Manor Farm.

It would be wrong not to mention another account of Gus' service during the early months of the war which first appeared in Gordon Campbell's book 'My Mystery Ships' but has been widely quoted since. Campbell describes how Gus was in Antwerp at the outbreak of war, joined the Belgian Army, was removed as a suspected person and returned to England where he volunteered for the RNVR. He goes on to say that Gus then returned to Antwerp as a Petty Officer with the RND, didn't want to be interned with the rest of the Division and so found himself a boat and got back to England where he was promptly dispatched to serve with the 10th Cruiser Squadron.

It has not been possible to find any documentary evidence to support this version of events. As detailed earlier in this chapter, Arthur Egerton Watts served with Gus during his training at the Crystal Palace and seems to suggest that Gus was under his command until he was commissioned into the RNR in December 1914. He makes no mention of Gus returning to Antwerp, neither does any of the official documentation relating to his service in the RNVR. Every newspaper account of Gus' life, prior to the publication of Gordon Campbell's book, says that he was in Antwerp when war broke out but make no mention that he returned there. Something else which would seem to suggest that Gus did not serve at Antwerp in the autumn of 1914 is the fact that amongst the medals which he was awarded at the end of the war is the 1914/15 Star. Had Gus served at Antwerp he would have been entitled to receive the 1914 Star.

TWO YEARS ON THE DRIFTERS.

Many books concerned with the history of the Great War give little consideration, if any, to the war at sea and those which do sometimes refer to it as a sideshow or a 'minor campaign.' Thousands of men, such as Gus, were to spend more than four years of their lives fighting a deadly enemy and trying to make sure that our island nation did not run out of food and vital supplies, whilst also attempting to ensure that the war effort could be maintained by the transportation of troops and the safe passage of all the materials needed to wage a war on land. For them, the war at sea was very much more than a sideshow.

The strategy of the British Navy in the Great War was to maintain British supply lines and to keep German ships in German ports and thereby prevent supplies reaching Germany. The strategy of the German Navy was to send U-boats to sink ships bringing supplies to the Allies; although this is of course a very

This photograph is believed to have been taken during the early years of the Great War when Gus was serving on the drifters at Larne. He is seated right.

simplified version of a complex situation. As will be seen in later chapters, the U-boat was a formidable enemy which came very close to winning the war for Germany.

Many different anti-submarine measures were introduced in an attempt to defeat the U-boat. Physical barriers to their passage such as nets and minefields were attempted, offensive strategies had to rely on various methods of trying to find a U-boat before it could be destroyed, and depth charges were not particularly accurate or effective during the early years of the war. In January 1915 Gus was sent to Falmouth to work on drifters: fishing vessels which had been taken over by the Navy and which were to have a variety of roles in the Great War. His pocket book reveals that on a date unknown he transferred to Larne, a few miles north-east of Belfast.

The aim of establishing a base at Larne was to deny enemy submarines passage down the Irish Sea. It was decided to barrage the north channel, the neck of water where north-east Ireland comes nearest to the west coast of Scotland. Hundreds of drifters towed special types of net into the channel with the basic intention of entangling a U-boat. The area which they had to cover was thirty miles by twenty-two and at each end armed patrols would cruise in the hope of catching any submarine which had managed to travel under the nets. Other bases were established at Milford, Kingstown and Liverpool and, with the net barrage and hundreds of patrols, it was hoped that U-boats would be deterred from entering the area. By the end of May 1915, Larne was home to one hundred and fifty net-drifters and 1,500 men who worked day and night in all weathers trying to maintain the barrage. In September 1915 Gus wrote:

> "We are getting a hell of a time up here just now with the weather and
> are like a lot of drowned rats most of time. Am at present trying to get

to Larne from the Mull against a S-Easter(sic) doing about one knot an
hour ahead and three toward the Atlantic."

On another occasion he wrote to his sister saying:

"Please excuse the awful scrawl but the ship is welling about something
devilish behind a rock in a south-easterly gale."

In his letters he refers to his sister, who was actually almost ten years his junior, as 'dear old Doll' and seems
to be very protective of her. Jane Bonner's letters to Dolly show that Gus regularly sent money home with
the instruction that some of it should be forwarded to his sister in Salonika.

ROMANCE IN THE AIR.

In January 1916 Jane wrote that Gus was expected home on leave, a leave which proved to be short but
eventful. In June 1914 Gus' eldest sister, Kitty, had married Thomas Herbert Partridge (Bert), a Walsall
solicitor and at some time during the early years of the war Gus had become friendly with Bert's sister
Alice Partridge, who was known as Cissy. Jane Bonner wrote that in the course of his three days leave, Gus
had spent some time at Minstead, the Partridge family home in Walsall and as soon as he left to go back
to sea he wrote to tell his parents that he and Cissy were engaged. Jane told Dolly:

"The day after Gus went back we had a letter from him saying he was
engaged to Cissy P. and that he was very fond of her. I rather suspected
it would take place this time home. I hope that they will be happy, but I
can't think that they will get on. They are both so determined and I fear
Mrs P. will make mischief."

Mrs P. was Cissy's mother. The following week Cissy visited her future in-laws to show them her
engagement ring. Jane wrote:

"It is regulation five diamonds, very small but looks good. She said Gus
wanted her to have a larger one but she thought that it would do."

In July 1916, Gus experienced a distressing incident whilst on board ship but it was not a submarine or the
weather which gave him concern, it was his health. He found himself completely unable to move and had
to be carried from the ship to the hospital, where he was diagnosed as having rheumatic fever. Somehow
by the time the news got back to England the story had become distorted and someone asked Cissy if it
was true that Mr Bonner, the sailor, was dead. Jane said:

"Cis could not speak. She simply fell back and gasped."

Gus, writing from his hospital bed, said that he was not very ill and was hoping to be granted a few days
leave when he left hospital, no doubt hoping to spend some time with his fiancée. Unfortunately his hopes
were dashed because as soon as he left hospital another officer was admitted with a shoulder injury and
Gus was needed back on duty. He told his mother that the situation was very bad, the Irish Sea being full
of U-boats and the mines they had laid.

Jane Bonner suggested to Dolly that Gus might not be able to send any more money because he would be
needing to save for the future but Gus had other ideas. He wrote:

"Send Dolly as much money as she wants and let me know if you have
enough for her but be sure to tell her not to be stingy! Expect she will
marry some Naval Officer who will be able to allow me £50 a year bye
and bye!"

It would appear that the subject of romance was very firmly in Gus' mind in the summer of 1916. Not only was he making comments about Dolly marrying a naval officer, he was also trying to marry his sister Mary to a friend of his, a fellow officer at Larne. He wrote to tell his mother that he hoped that they would marry but his attempts at playing matchmaker were not very successful: his friend writing a four page letter to Mary extolling the virtues of the girl he had left at home!

In the autumn of 1916, Gus came home on leave, spending his time walking in the leafy lanes around Aldridge with Cissy, taking her to the theatre (with chaperone of course) and attending a family gathering at Manor Farm, presumably held to introduce Cissy to the extended Bonner clan. However Gus' leave was cut short when he received word that he had to return to duty. The battle against the U-boats was soon to enter a new phase and one which would prove decisive. A change at the Admiralty at the end of 1916 saw Sir John Jellicoe appointed as First Sea Lord, one of his first decisions being to set up an Anti-Submarine Division with the aim of co-ordinating existing measures and developing new ones. As the year ended, as he waited to learn what part he might play in the changing situation, Gus was promoted to Lieutenant with a seniority date of 23rd December 1916.

Germany had declared unrestricted U-boat warfare three times during the first half of the war but on each occasion they had 'backed off,' mainly due to pressure from America, a topic which will be considered further in the next chapter. The year ahead was to be the defining year in the battle against Germany's U-boat and the most dramatic of Gus' life. At the beginning of February 1917, Germany took the make or break decision to give the order that any vessel of any nation found in the waters around Britain, France, Italy or the Eastern Mediterranean was liable to be sunk without warning. It was to be their most successful campaign of unrestricted U-boat warfare and one which would bring the Allies perilously close to defeat. Gus left Larne to return to Devonport to await new instructions and was still there on March 9th when he wrote to his parents:

"Sorry to say, most of the Larne boys were sent to Portsmouth as the
barracks here were too crowded. I suppose Cis told you I'm living in
the barracks now, much nicer. Large room and fire and all
conveniences at hand. The C.O. here is economising by allowing
us only six envelopes and sheets of paper. Expect I shall manage
to do my average correspondence on them."

Amongst the Bonner family's personal papers is a letter from the son of the man who commanded a fleet of drifters at Larne during the early years of the war. He writes:

" I can remember as a small boy, Bonner's drifters being cheered
away as he left to join the Q-ships."

Compared to most of the lads Gus grew up with in Aldridge, his life had already been quite exciting, but 1917 was to see him face dangers and receive honours that he could have scarce imagined. The man who had described himself as a selfish pig in that letter of Christmas 1913 would soon be known to the nation as a hero.

Chapter 3
QUEENSTOWN AND THE Q-SHIPS

In the Spring of 1917, Gus arrived in Queenstown, Southern Ireland, to join the Q-ship service and we will return to his story later. However, in order to understand the chapters which are to follow, it is important to have some understanding of what Q-ships were, why they were needed, how they operated and of their connection with Queenstown.

Queenstown, a naval base in Southern Ireland now renamed Cobh, had a very large natural harbour (which it is said could have accommodated the entire British Fleet) and an excellent naval dockyard on one of its islands, Haulbowline. Queenstown was something of a quiet backwater at the outbreak of war. With the British Grand Fleet virtually imprisoning the German High Seas Fleet, no one believed that any German ship would break out into the wide ocean; nor did anyone imagine that German U-boats had the capability to travel as far as the south of Ireland. In 1914 Queenstown looked destined to play a minor role in the war but at the end of January 1915 a German U-boat, U21, came through the English Channel into the Irish Sea, passing both Holyhead and Liverpool before opening fire on an air-ship shed at Barrow-in-Furness. On their return they attacked three steamers just off the Mersey. U21 was to be the first of many.

Despite the Allies best efforts, Germany continued to send her U-boats into British waters until the end of the war. Over the next four years many different anti-submarine measures would be employed, with varying degrees of success. These included fixed and floating obstructions, mines, patrols, Q-ships (described in detail later in this chapter), armed merchant vessels, submarines, the use of hydrophones, air patrols and P-boats: fast, low-lying shallow draft boats, difficult to see at distance and fitted with steel to act as a ram.

In May 1915, Queenstown became a familiar name throughout the world as the town which received both the living and the dead from one of the most famous U-boat incidents of all time: the sinking of the 32,000 ton Cunard liner *Lusitania*. A few months earlier, Germany had decreed that as from February 18th all waters around Great Britain and Ireland would be considered a war zone and that any vessel found to be in the area was liable to be sunk without warning. The German embassy in Washington made announcements in New York newspapers to that effect but no one believed that a prestigious liner like the *Lusitania* would ever be a target. They were wrong. On May 7th, a torpedo fired by U20 hit the ship, causing her to sink within approximately twenty minutes. Vessels were dispatched from Queenstown, returning with the living, the dead and the dying, whilst the political fall-out threatened to bring America into the war on the side of the Allies. The news that bodies of women and children were floating in the Irish Sea and that the streets of Queenstown were full of relatives inspecting rows of corpses or desperately seeking news of a loved one, must have had a profound effect on people such as Gus who were engaged in attempting to defeat the U-boats. Almost 1,200 of the 1,959 people onboard the *Lusitania* lost their lives. Any remnants of the so called 'chivalry of the sea' was surely at an end.

THE ARRIVAL OF LEWIS BAYLY.

Almost overnight Queenstown changed from a sleepy little backwater into an important base from which to organise a defence against the U-boat, the man to do the organising being fifty-eight year old Vice-Admiral Sir Lewis Bayly KCB CVO, president of the Royal Naval College, Greenwich, who had seen

Queenstown Harbour.
(Courtesy of the Imperial War Museum, London. Q14902)

active service earlier in the war. Lewis Bayly has been described by many of the people who served with him during the Great War as: clear-thinking, loyal, independently minded, patriotic, modest, sympathetic, direct and having an extraordinary ability to focus on the job he had to do and of employing every means possible to reach his goal. He brought with him his niece, Violet Voysey, who was to act as his companion, housekeeper and P.A. for the rest of the war and beyond.

For those who were used to the much more leisurely pace of life of Queenstown, the arrival of Lewis Bayly must have come as quite a shock. Under his command there were to be no more social calls and to make the point he gave over part of his private quarters to be used for naval business, asking the staff at Haulbowline to make a wooden cover for the billiard table so that he could use it to map the positions of his ships. The only entertaining he intended to do was with the captains of his ships and, for them, both he and Admiralty House would be available twenty-four hours a day. He wanted to get to know each of them, understand their strengths and difficulties and thereby mount the most efficient and effective campaign possible against the U-boat menace.

But in Queenstown's case her enemies came from the land as well as the sea, with many disaffected Irishmen believing that the future for their homeland would be better served by a German victory in the Great War. The Admiralty had warned Lewis Bayly that valuable information about naval operations was getting into enemy hands and so he ordered a number of changes to improve security.

Existing rows of buildings rose up steeply from Queenstown harbour and so any signals sent from Admiralty House on the hill could readily be seen from below. Bayly ordered a new signal station to be built on Haulbowline and, as an added precaution, ordered that all important signals were to be encoded. He

*Lewis Bayly.
This photograph was
taken after his
promotion to Admiral
in 1917.*

was also aware that any friction between the Navy and the Roman Catholic church in Queenstown could cause unnecessary difficulties, so he approached the Bishop and suggested that they should work together. The Most Reverend Robert Browne agreed and so began a friendship which would last well beyond the end of the war.

An example of how serious the security threat was came in April 1916 when Lewis Bayly received a warning that Germany was planning to land arms in support of an Irish Easter uprising. At this time of heightened tension, a signal station reported a steamer acting suspiciously. Lewis Bayly was taking no chances: he ordered that she be followed and boarded. Although nothing untoward was found, he gave orders that the ship, the Aud, be brought into Queenstown and, if she resisted, to sink her! He describes standing on the verandah of Admiralty House watching her being escorted in:

> "Suddenly the *Aud* stopped, hoisted two German naval ensigns and
> lowered her boats, into which got the officers and seamen - about
> thirty in number - in (German) naval uniform. Then an explosion
> occurred on the *Aud* and she went to the bottom! It transpired that the
> Captain thought that he had sunk her in the channel and that she would
> be a nuisance to me, but this was not so."

The ship was a German auxiliary cruiser, disguised to look like a Norwegian tramp steamer. Divers were sent down and came back with rifles, machine guns, munitions etc; the rifles being Russian and probably captured by the Germans at the beginning of the war. The divers also retrieved a German ensign which Lewis Bayly had framed and displayed on the wall of Admiralty House. In 1936 he returned it to the German Navy, the Admiral who received it replying:

> "I see it (the return of the ensign) as a renewed proof of the friendly
> relations which bind our two Navies together in mutual respect."

WHAT WAS A Q-SHIP?

Put simply, a Q-ship was a man-of-war which pretended to be a merchant ship. She looked and behaved like a merchant ship but had concealed guns and a highly trained crew who sprang into action as soon as they encountered a U-boat; their aim being to convince the U-boat crew that they were of little threat, thereby inducing them to approach. A wide variety of vessels were fitted as Q-ships, including tramp-steamers, colliers, smacks, steam trawlers, schooners and P-boats. Several writers have offered suggestions as to why such

*One of the
smaller Q-ships,
HMS 'Eilian'
with her gun screens
in place.*

'Eilian' after her
gun-screens had gone
overboard in heavy
weather.

vessels were called Q-ships: one theory being that they were so called because they operated out of Queenstown but, as they also operated from other areas, this explanation does not hold water. A more plausible suggestion is that Q was simply a letter which the Admiralty gave to this particular type of ship; other names which were used included decoy ship, mystery ship or special service ship. For their part the Germans called them trap-ships. The idea was not a new one, in fact such vessels had been in use in one form or another for more than 200 years; however the Great War was to see the use of Q-ships implemented as official Admiralty policy for the first time.

During the early years of the war merchant ships which were to be converted for Q-ship service were chosen by the Admiralty, however the selections did not always prove popular with the men who had to take them to sea, or with Lewis Bayly. Speaking of two such ships, Lewis Bayly remarked:

> "They were much too large and laden with coal. The only apparent
> use for the coal was to enable them to sink at once if torpedoed, and
> so save the crew from the trouble and discomfort of trying to prolong
> their lives by staying on board."

He managed to persuade the Admiralty that his captains should be allowed to select vessels which they thought suitable for conversion and to have them taken to Devonport or brought to Haulbowline for the re-fit.

On arrival at the dockyard the chosen ship would be photographed and plans made for the most suitable positions for the hidden guns; then the work of dismantling her would begin. By this stage of the war it was normal practice for merchant ships to be fitted with a clearly visible defensive gun in a usually vain attempt to fight back against the U-boat, although the Admiralty was somewhat reluctant to provide such guns. In the case of Gus' first Q-ship, HMS *Pargust*, the refusal to provide a defensive gun led her commander, Gordon Campbell, to have a dummy made. A Q-ship's defensive gun was the only one which was visible, all of the others being concealed behind various structures. Once the guns were in place, the hold filled with wood to aid buoyancy, various structures made moveable or collapsible and a voice-pipe fitted to enable the captain to communicate with his men (the reasons for which will be explained later), the ship was restored to her former appearance. Photographs would again be taken and compared to the earlier ones, ensuring that she looked exactly as she had on entering the dockyard. This may sound like a fairly straightforward job, but it is important to remember that not only did the guns need to be concealed in various places but they also had to be capable of being uncovered immediately they were needed. As will be shown in subsequent chapters, the window of opportunity for a Q-ship to fire on a U-boat could be both infrequent and narrow, making it vital that they were seized upon when they presented themselves.

UNRESTRICTED U-BOAT WAR.

Although Germany was waging a successful war against merchant shipping at the beginning of 1917, they were facing huge pressures to step up their campaign and end the war sooner rather than later. The German people were suffering from the Royal Navy's blockade of their country, some estimates suggesting that as many as 700,000 Germans died as a result of hunger or the inability to fight disease brought on by malnutrition during the Great War. Admiral Scheer, newly acclaimed as a hero of the German Navy following the Battle of Jutland, warned that Germany was very likely to face defeat if her Navy attempted to engage the British Grand Fleet again. He saw the intensification of the U-boat war as Germany's best chance of victory.

The major drawback to an unrestricted U-boat campaign was the very real danger that it could bring the United States of America into the war. Germany decided to take the risk, believing that if they could sink their monthly target of 600,000 tons of shipping during the early months of such a campaign, the Allies would be forced to use most of their available shipping to maintain essential supplies. This, they reasoned, would leave precious few ships to transport American troops to the front-line, meaning that the war would effectively be over before they could be used in France and Flanders in large numbers. Germany also believed that neutral shipping would be paralysed by the U-boat menace and when their campaign began it looked as though their calculation that unrestricted submarine warfare would end the war in Germany's favour within six months, was likely to be correct.

It may be remembered that two months before the war began, Gus was on the steamer *Incemore* which collided with the German liner *Kaiser Wilhelm II* in the Solent. Both vessels were to play a part in the fight against the U-boat: *Incemore* being torpedoed without warning and sunk on 20th August and the liner, which had been in American waters when the war began, being converted to a troop transporter and eventually employed in carrying American troops to the front line.

On January 31st 1917, Germany announced that as from February 1st all navigation around the coast of Britain, adjacent to France and Italy and in the Eastern Mediterranean was prohibited, and that any vessel of any nation found in these waters would be sunk without warning. On the first day of the campaign a small tramp steamer was sunk with the loss of ten lives and, by the end of February, U-boats had destroyed eighty-six ships out of a total loss of more than a hundred for the month; worse was to come. Within a few days of the declaration of unrestricted U-boat warfare America severed diplomatic relations with Germany and ordered the German Ambassador to leave the embassy in Washington. There was evidence that embassy personnel had been liasing between their homeland, the disaffected Irish and their sympathisers in America, thus their removal made an Irish uprising less likely. This was one small piece of good news in what were very difficult times.

METHOD OF OPERATION.

As in any conflict, the strategy of the Q-ships changed and adapted throughout the war. The following description concerns the method of operation of such ships, operating out of Queenstown from February 1917, the month in which Germany started her campaign of unrestricted submarine warfare, and the month before Gus joined his first Q-ship.

Commander Gordon Campbell, the man who Gus was to serve under, had studied the ever-changing tactics of the U-boats, deciding that under the current climate in which torpedoes could be fired without warning, the only chance for a Q-ship to successfully engage the enemy, was to not just allow herself to be torpedoed but to deliberately alter course to ensure that it happened! Sometimes, a Q-ship could be at sea for months on end without even seeing a U-boat let alone engaging one. If an enemy torpedo was fired at them but missed, they had to be seen to be behaving as an ordinary merchant vessel would have done and attempt to get away. By ensuring that the enemy torpedo hit, the Q-ship had an the opportunity to engage the enemy as planned.

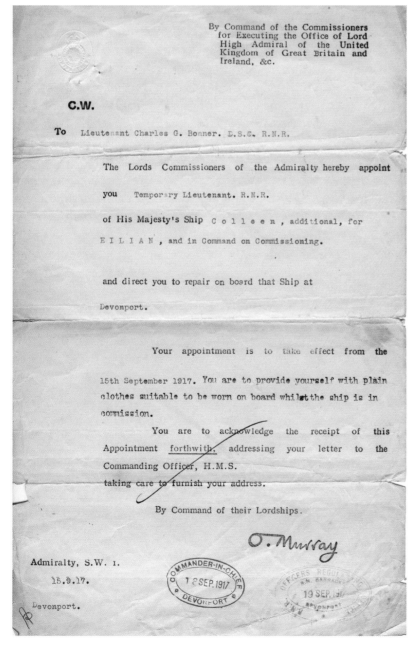

A letter appointing Gus to the third of his three Q-ships. Note the instruction that he was to provide himself with plain clothes.

The Q-ship's aim was to get the U-boat to surface and approach the ship: their hope always being that perhaps the U-boat had a limited supply of torpedoes which he preferred to save in case of 'bigger fish to fry.' If they could persuade a U-boat captain that they were a harmless merchant ship, not worth another of his torpedoes, then he might close in and present them with an opportunity to open fire; if not he could send them to the sea-bed. Of course, there was absolutely no prospect of convincing a U-boat captain that he was dealing with a merchant ship if all the men on board wore naval uniform and adhered to naval discipline and vocabulary, so the officers and men of the Q-ships slouched about their ship, used the language of a merchant seaman such as Skipper instead of Captain etc. and received an allowance of thirty shillings to provide their own clothes Many writers have described them as actors and whilst this is a fitting analogy, it should be remembered that the majority of the men who served on His Majesty's Q-ships belonged to the RNR and that many, like Gus, had previously lived the life of a merchant seaman for a number of years.

Rear-Admiral William Sims of the United States Navy appeared to be quite shocked when he witnessed the transformation from smart naval men to rough and ready seafarers, saying:

> "A more villainous-looking gang of seaman than the crews of these
> ships never sailed the waves. All men on board were naval officers
> or enlisted men; all volunteers, and comprised men of all ranks.
> All had temporarily abandoned His Majesty's uniform for garments
> picked up in second-hand clothing stores."

Below decks things were very different. A Q-ship carried up to three times more men than she would have done during her days as a merchant vessel, needing to ensure that she was always in a permanent state of readiness, with all guns manned. It was vital that good discipline was maintained in these overcrowded conditions and that the crew learned to accept orders from their officers, even if those officers were wearing an old donkey jacket and scruffy hat and not the smart naval uniform to which they would normally give due deference.

On leaving Queenstown harbour for the first time, one of the initial considerations for a Q-ship captain was whether anyone had managed to breach security or become suspicious of the 'strange comings and goings' during the preparations for his ship's new role. In order to allow for that possibility, the ship was changed in some way as soon as she left harbour: masts might be altered, coloured boards slotted onto her sides, dummy funnels put in place or stanchions and structures moved around on deck, thus enabling the ship to take on a quite different appearance.

Once a Q-ship was in open water she could not just 'hang around' waiting to catch the eye of a U-boat captain; that would only attract suspicion. Merchant vessels were always travelling from one place to another and so, during daylight hours, a Q-ship would need to appear to be on a set course. However if she actually completed a journey between one place and another, she would waste a lot of time in areas where there was no U-boat activity. And so each night, under cover of darkness, the crew would again alter the appearance of their vessel, just as they had done when they left harbour. This meant that they had to work very long hours; in the next chapter Gus describes their hours of work as:

> "Some 24 hours a day with an addition for longitude when steaming west!"

A typical routine for the Q-ship men was eight days at sea followed by four days in harbour. This might appear to be quite generous but it should be remembered that their days at sea were long and lived in a permanent state of heightened tension. No one was conscripted to the service, all of the men were volunteers and rightly so. It has often been said of them that any one man could 'spoil the show.' It is not too dramatic a statement to say that they relied on each other for their lives not just in some grand way at the height of a battle but also in the minute details of the drama as it unfolded, and at no time was that more evident than when, perhaps after many months at sea, they heard the words, 'torpedo approaching.' In that instant they knew that this was likely to be a fight to the death and that each of them could influencethe outcome, some in a quiet way by simply playing their part to perfection, others in a more dramatic fashion.

Having made the necessary adjustments to the speed and position of his ship to ensure that the torpedo would impact where it would do the least damage, the captain would order the defensive gun to return fire and send a dummy message for urgent assistance, 'forgetting' to give his position. Such a message had to be sent as it would be expected from a merchant ship who came under fire. Eventually came the order, 'Abandon Ship.' The U-boat commander would be aware that his torpedo had hit the target but would be too far distant to know what degree of damage had been inflicted. It was at this stage that the men were called upon to use their acting skills, convincing the enemy that their ship had been dealt a devastating blow and that the only option left to them was to abandon ship. Those on deck would rush around in a state of panic and a few from below decks would emerge as though woken from their sleep to see what all the noise was about. One man might suddenly decide that he had forgotten to rescue the ship's cat, rushing back to search for it, whilst all the time their aim was to delay as long as possible, drawing the U-boat ever closer to their ship. Then they would gather a few belongings together before taking to the lifeboats; the navigating officer taking on the role of skipper and having one more look around 'his' vessel, perhaps going below to collect some 'important papers' and then eventually joining the rest of the men in the lifeboats. This group was referred to as the 'panic' or 'abandon ship' party and always consisted of the same number of men as would have been onboard at the time the vessel was an innocent merchant ship.

Some of the men of the Q-ship 'Eilian.' Despite their appearance these men were highly trained members of His Majesty's naval forces.

The role of the 'abandon ship' party was not an easy one, as they had to act as frightened merchant seaman whilst actually knowing that the success or failure of the battle could rely on their ability to behave as disciplined and fearless navy men. Once they were in the lifeboats their job was to lure the U-boat to within range of the Q-ship's guns by playing the part of incompetent or frightened oarsman and making no headway. If they aroused any suspicion they could find themselves under fire but, if they could play their part to full effect, they might be able to induce a U-boat to close in to see what was going on or perhaps lead the enemy to a position on which the Q-ship's guns could be brought to bear. If all else failed they might be required to head back towards the ship, acting as though they intended to board her again. This, according to one eye-witness account, made the Germans very cross indeed. The 'abandon ship' party was in a very vulnerable position against a powerful enemy and it comes as no surprise that many of those involved were decorated or mentioned in dispatches as a result of their bravery, although none were awarded the VC.

A U-boat might circle a torpedoed vessel for several hours: looking for any signs of life before closing in for the kill and so it was vital that those left on board remained motionless in order to convince the enemy that she was abandoned. No matter how uncomfortable the position in which they found themselves after the torpedo struck, no matter if the ship was on fire or sinking, their orders were to stay out of sight and await their captain's instructions. The captain, from his look out position, would be watching the submarine like a hawk and speaking to his crew via a voice-pipe: it being vital that he could order 'open fire' as soon as an opportunity presented itself. That opportunity came when the U-boat was on the surface, within range, with her conning tower open and when as many guns as possible could bear: this being the only time which the Q-ship might have the upper hand. Then the captain would raise the White Ensign (to show that she was a naval ship) and give the order to open fire, with those in the panic party having to jump into the sea if they found themselves in the firing line!

Of course things didn't always go to plan If a Q-ship was so badly damaged that there was absolutely no prospect of 'putting up a fight,' the captain's responsibility was to do what he could to save his men, ordering all of them to take to the lifeboats. But here lay another problem: how could they explain why there were so many men onboard? The explanation which was to be given to an inquisitive U-boat commander, should he approach them, was that some onboard had been picked up as survivors from another vessel which had struck a mine. In order for the bluff to work, and possibly save their lives, each man, to use the acting analogy again, would have to 'learn his lines' which were posted on blackboards around the ship. As has already been mentioned, a Q-ship would change both course and appearance overnight and so three sets of lines had to be learnt. Several questions were anticipated. What is the name of your ship and where was it registered? Who is the owner and what is the name of your captain? What is your tonnage and cargo? Which port did you leave and when? Where are you headed? In addition, those who were playing the part of the ship-wrecked crew of the fictitious mined vessel would need to know when and where they were supposed to have struck a mine and how many men were onboard at the time.

The lives of the Q-ship men depended upon several variable factors: on the U-boat captain being prepared to use methods other than a torpedo to destroy their ship, on the panic party doing all they could to manoeuvre the U-boat into a suitable position, on those left on board remaining motionless, on their ship not sinking or being destroyed by fire and on the captain recognising his best possible opportunity to open fire and taking it. If they did have to completely abandon ship, each relied on the other to have 'learnt their lines' and so not give the game away if questioned. The odds were not in their favour, as is borne out by the statistics which show that in such encounters more Q-ships than U-boats were destroyed.

GORDON CAMPBELL VC.

At the beginning of 1917 Gus began his training for service on His Majesty's Q-ships, having met a Q-ship captain at Devonport who saw something in him which he said made him, "cut out for the job." There was always a waiting list of men wanting to join; some being attracted by better pay and longer leave, whilst others were looking for adventure or simply enjoyed the unconventional nature of the work.

The Devonport captain who recommended Gus was Commander Gordon Campbell DSO RN, one of the most famous naval men of the Great War. He was a year younger than Gus and had begun his naval career in 1900 as a cadet, joining his first ship, the *Prince George*, as a midshipman in 1902. By the time that he and Gus met, Gordon Campbell was already a Q-ship veteran whom Admiral Bayly described as:

"A born leader of men with a wonderful sense of duty to his country."

Rear-Admiral Sims said of him:

"Had the Naval war taken the course of most Naval wars, Campbell would probably have served well but perhaps not brilliantly. This conflict, however, demanded a new type of warfare and, at the same time, demanded a new type of Naval fighter. To go hunting for the submarine, required not only courage of a high order, but analytical intelligence, patience and a talent for preparation and detail. Captain Campbell seemed to have been created for this particular task"

Gordon Campbell had been awarded the Distinguished Service Order following an action in March 1916 which saw his Q-ship *Farnborough* sink U68 off the west coast of Ireland. A month before Gus joined the Q-ship service, Commander Campbell became the first of eight Q-ship men to receive the Victoria Cross.

On February 17th 1917, after eight days at sea in his ship *Farnborough* (now called *Q5*) a torpedo was sighted. On impact the sea began to flood the ship and by the time the panic party had took to the lifeboats, *Q5* was settling by the stern. Although he had a number of opportunities to fire on the U-boat as it surfaced to examine the ship and lifeboats, Campbell held his nerve and waited until he could bring all guns to bear before opening fire at point blank range. The first shot decapitated the German captain as a total of forty-five shells rained down on U83.Two survivors were rescued, but *Q5* was in a bad way. Campbell then sent what is now a much quoted message to Lewis Bayly. It said:

"*Q5* slowly sinking respectfully wishes you goodbye."

Fortunately assistance was at hand and Campbell and his crew were taken on board HMS *Narwhal*. No doubt mindful of the nation's need for shipping, he returned to *Q5* with twelve of his officers and men, whilst HMS *Buttercup* attempted to tow her. After losing the tow several times and with the waves breaking over the deck Campbell ordered his men to get into a waiting motor-boat and took a final look around his ship. What happened next is hard to believe. The sudden explosion of an on-board depth charge sent Campbell scurrying for the motor-boat but their ordeal was far from over. The towing ship, thinking that the explosion had been caused by a torpedo fired from a U-boat, slipped the tow and returned to Queenstown, reporting that Campbell and his men were probably dead. They were not dead but they were drifting around in dangerous waters at the coldest time of year in a mal-functioning motor-boat. Thankfully they were rescued by HMS *Laburnum*, yet Campbell had still not given up on his ship and returned to her deck twice more before eventually managing to beach her at Mill Cove, close to Ireland's most southerly tip.

For his 'conspicuous gallantry, consummate coolness and skill in command of one of HM ships in action,' Gordon Campbell was awarded the Victoria Cross. *Q5* was badly damaged and when Campbell chose a new ship, HMS *Pargust*, the newly-trained Gus joined him as second officer.

HOPE ON THE HORIZON.

Lieutenant Charles George Bonner RNR. The design of the braid which Royal Naval Reserve officers wore on their sleeves resulted in them being known as 'the Chain Gang.'

Although the first month of unrestricted U-boat warfare had brought heavy losses, the month of March 1917 saw even greater loss of merchant shipping and by April totals were exceeding even Germany's most optimistic expectations with 860,334 tons of shipping being sunk in just one month. In his history of the Great War, author Liddell Hart stated that during April 1917, one ship out of every four that left the British Isles never came home; Winston Churchill describing the area to the south-west of Ireland as a veritable cemetery of British shipping. It was suggested that the Navy was in danger of losing the war before the Army had chance to win it.

However, in the midst of great losses of both shipping and life (a thousand lives lost in April alone), came the first glimmer of hope for the Allies. The idea of using convoys for merchant shipping had been the subject of on-going debate. They were already used to ensure the safety of troops crossing to the battlefields but had not been used to any great extent for merchant shipping because of opposition of both the Navy and the owners and masters of the ships. The essence of the convoy system was that a group of ships, around twenty in number (although this varied), would travel together and be protected by a naval escort when they reached the areas in which they were vulnerable to U-boat attack. The Navy had resisted the system because they had a limited number of destroyers and did not want to use them for escort work. Ship owners and masters were also opposed to the idea, arguing that a convoy could only travel at the speed of the slowest vessel and that because it was difficult to maintain position in convoy, vessels could be damaged. They also argued that ports would become very congested with so many ships arriving at the same time. But their overwhelming objection was that when shipping was spread out across the seas at least some of them stood a chance of avoiding an encounter with a U-boat, whilst a convoy was seen as just one big target for a submarine commander. However, desperate times called for desperate measures and so, in April 1917, it was decided to give the convoy system a thorough trial.

April saw another development which was to change life at Queenstown: America's patience had finally run out. The American people were very unhappy about the campaign of unrestricted U-boat warfare and when they were given the news that Germany had attempted to forge an alliance with Mexico in the so called Zimmerman telegram, the nation was outraged. Addressing Congress to outline his case for declaring war against Germany, President Woodrow Wilson said:

> "The present German submarine warfare against commerce is a warfare
> against mankind. It is a warfare against all nations."

He argued that Germany had removed America's choice to be neutral, saying that his country would not choose the path of submission. He said:

> "Right is more precious than peace."

On April 7th 1917 America announced that it was at war with Germany. Lewis Bayly was summoned to the Admiralty and told that American destroyers would be arriving at Queenstown in May and that they would be put under his orders. He wrote:

> "The Admiralty hoped that I would be nice to them. On my way back
> to Queenstown I wondered how to be 'nice' to them and finally
> decided to treat them exactly the way I treated the British."

On the afternoon of April 24th the destroyers slipped quietly out of Boston and made their way to a position fifty miles east of Cape Cod: the officer in charge, Captain Taussig, being given instructions to open a sealed envelope when they got there. The orders told him that their assistance had been requested by the Admiralty in the task of protecting commerce near the coasts of Great Britain and France and that they were to make their way to Queenstown. On arrival at their destination, the six American captains reported to Lewis Bayly as instructed. He shook hands with each one of them and then asked when their ships would be ready to put to sea. Captain Taussig had been warned that Bayly was a 'no nonsense' leader and so his response to the question was straight to the point:

> "Ready as soon as we are fuelled, Sir."

They were then invited to stay for dinner at Admiralty House and some of them stayed the night. The following morning Lewis Bayly met with all six of them and, before explaining the current situation and what their duties would involve, he began by saying:

"Gentlemen, the Admiralty are afraid I shall be rude to you. I shan't
if you do your work; I shall if you don't."

So began a level of understanding and co-operation which would last for the rest of the war and beyond, as each newly arrived American captain was welcomed with the same mix of warm hospitality and plain speaking; Admiral Bayly being affectionately known to most American sailors as 'Uncle Lewis' though not to his face of course! Over the next few months thirty-five American destroyers would make the long trip to Queenstown and by the end of the year more than a quarter of all convoy escorts would come from the USA. It would appear that the man who was charged with the command of America's naval forces, Rear-Admiral William Sims, had a great deal in common with Lewis Bayly: they were of a similar age, outspoken, practical, dedicated and well respected by the officers and men under their command. William Sims, who later went on to command America's naval forces throughout Europe, found himself at odds with some of his superiors who disapproved of his belief in the need for American forces to integrate with the British. In a letter to Gus dated 4th June 1920, he spoke of the errors committed by the Navy Department in the Great War concluding:

" I believe that there is nothing more beneficial to a military organisation
than drastic criticism after the event. All the military organisations
during the war doubtless made mistakes, and these should be thoroughly
ventilated so that they may not be made again."

The early months of 1917 had been eventful for everyone at Queenstown but Germany still had the upper hand. When Gus Bonner's first Q-ship, HMS *Pargust*, left port to play her part in the battle, her crew were well aware of the importance and danger of the work they were doing; much would be asked of them in the next few months.

Chapter 4
PARGUST: A CLASSIC ENCOUNTER

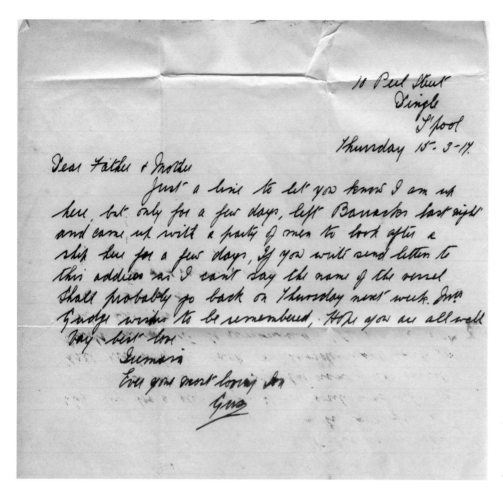

*The letter which
Gus sent to his
parents to tell
them that he was
'looking after
a ship.'*

The precise date on which Gus joined the Q-ship HMS *Pargust* is unclear. His conduct certificate, a copy of which is included in the next chapter, states that he joined *Pargust* on March 10th 1917, although the date on the document does appear to have been altered. On Thursday March 15th he wrote to inform his parents that he was in Liverpool with a group of men, looking after a ship whose name he could not divulge. Whilst he was there Cissy went up to see him, accompanied by her mother of course: it would not have been seemly for a young woman to visit her fiancé without a chaperone.

At the beginning of April Gus wrote to say that he was in Glasgow with a group of men 'looking at a ship' and it is possible that both his visit to Glasgow and his previous visit to Liverpool had been for the purpose of inspecting ships which might have been suitable for Q-ship service. On his way back from Scotland to Devonport, Gus was given permission to break his journey and take a few days leave. This gave him the opportunity of meeting his new nephew, Thomas Michael Partridge, Kitty and Bert's first child who had been born in January and, of course, to spend time with Cissy. Gus was quite clearly in love and no sooner had he returned to Devonport, than Cissy and Mrs P followed him to spend a few more precious hours together. He wrote to tell his parents that he wished that he had married her during his last leave, adding that they should arrange for the ceremony to take place during his next leave, although he could not say when that might be!

At the end of May, Jane wrote to tell her daughters that their brother had met with an accident. She wrote:

> "Gus has evidently met with an accident or something as soon as they got out (presumably out to sea). This boat was the *Vittoria* and they had been getting her ready for weeks. He says in his letter they have transferred to the *Pargust* (it was actually the same ship, only the name had changed) but he cannot tell us anything about it, but hopes to one day. Cissy seems to think they have caught a sub, but I think it is the other way round."

The details of Gus' 'accident' are not known although it is possible that it may have occurred on his way to Queenstown.

HIS OWN ACCOUNT.

In 1930, Gus wrote an account of the action between HMS *Pargust* and the mine laying submarine, UC 29, for the journal of Furness Withy, one of his former employers. Although he would later be awarded the Distinguished Service Cross for his bravery, the article does not mention his own role in the action. His account, which is published here in full, reveals something of his character: his subtle sense of humour and irony, his 'matter of fact' attention to detail, his modesty and his admiration for the men with whom he served. It is reproduced here as it was written, save for the words in brackets which have been added by way of explanation.

The SS 'Vittoria' in Clifton Gorge, Bristol, prior to her re-fit as the Q-ship HMS 'Pargust.'
(Image No. P88.1. Courtesy of Amgueddfa Cymru-National Museum Wales).

"The *Pargust*, whose previous name was the S.S. *Vittoria*, of Cardiff, of 2,817 gross, was taken over by the Admiralty and placed in Plymouth Dockyard for conversion into a Mystery or Special Service Ship at the end of March 1917, under the command of Commander Gordon Campbell VC DSO, now Rear-

42

Admiral, whose previous vessel, the *Loderer*, (also called *Q5* or *Farnborough*) had suffered so severely in her last successful engagement with a German Submarine as to be definitely out of commission for some months. The arrangements for arming a vessel with five or six guns, torpedo tubes, depth charges, and other weapons, and at the same time preserve her character of an ordinary common or garden merchant ship were not jobs to be undertaken light-heartedly in a few minutes, and much careful thought had to be given to the position of each weapon, and to its most efficient disguise. The disguised position of the guns had to be strong enough to stand the shock to be expected from a torpedo exploding near it without revealing the gun, and at the same time handy enough to be shed instantaneously when the moment to open fire arrived.

Campbell, after his great successes and experiences in command of the *Loderer*, was a past master in the art of disguise, and also encouraged his officers and men to come forward with any ideas for improvements, with the result that new and clever gadgets were always being improvised. The disguise of each Mystery Ship was left entirely to its Commander and, generally Campbell stuck to the disguises which he had tried out in the *Loderer* and which brought him through three successful engagements in that vessel. As the submarine war progressed, however, the prospects of the Mystery Ship pulling off a successful action considerably diminished, partly because any ship not in convoy was an object of suspicion to the German Submarine Commander, and also because the Germans had learnt to fear a close attack by gunfire for fear of meeting a tartar. The *Pargust*, therefore, was fitted out to be torpedoed as that, in her Commanders opinion, was the only way to bag the enemy.

Four additional W.T.(watertight) bulkheads were put in, and her holds filled with wood, in order to keep her afloat for some time at any rate after being torpedoed. One twelve-pounder gun was built in abaft the windlass and lay flat on deck when not in action, being released when wanted, and springing into position by means of a heavy lead counter-balance. A similar gun emplacement was put on the after end of the house between the lifeboats. In the houses over the engine room, normally accommodating the engineers, one 12-pounder was placed each side, with a very handy disguise consisting of dropping the top half of the plating, which could be done instantaneously and the guns brought into action in three seconds. On the poop a four inch gun was concealed in various ways by hatch coamings, crates, derricks which flew up to the head of a Samson post when released, and other disguises. The torpedo tubes, one on each side, were placed in the shelter deck immediately under the bridge and could be fired from there as required, a small port opening automatically to allow the torpedo to get away on its job when released from the tube. The depth charges were placed in the poop on trays, having carefully concealed dropping ports cut in the stern to give them an exit. The remaining armament of machine guns, Lewis guns and bombs, were placed where thought necessary, and owing to their size were not difficult to hide.

On deck a large amount of spare gear with which to change the ship was carried, such as dummy donkey funnel, crosstrees for the lower mast heads, samson posts, extra derricks, hen houses etc., etc. All these preparations took time, and it was not until the last week in May that we proceeded into Plymouth Sound, and after 36 hours of intensive drilling, and trying out various disguise, our Commander being satisfied that everything was in order, sailed for Queenstown to report to the Commander-in-Chief there, Admiral Sir Lewis Bayly- that brilliant officer who, more than anyone in the Service, did so much to check the enemies' submarine activities- under whom our ship was to serve. On arrival at Queenstown on May 30th Admiral Sir Lewis Bayly inspected the ship, and we sailed the following night.

Practically all the Officers and crew had served under Campbell in his previous ship, otherwise the work of training would have been much more difficult, as, although we had a crew of some 80 men, the watch and station drill for action stations was necessarily complicated - with an abandon ship party to be sent away; the guns, torpedoes and depth charges to man - the course the action was likely to take had to be considered before some of the crew could be given definite stations. The Doctor, for instance, at sea spent most of his daylight hours walking the deck as a passenger and, incidentally, keeping a lookout, and, at night, took a watch at decoding. In action he was first Doctor; second, Official Photographer; third, one of the abandon ship party; whichever job he was ordered to when the time came.

HMS 'Pargust.'
(Image No. P88.5. Courtesy of Amgueddfa Cymru-National Museum Wales).

Our Commander's general tactics on this voyage were to steam out from the Fastnet to the Westward throughout the day, disguise the vessel throughout the night, and return toward the Irish Coast the following day, as submarines were playing havoc in this locality. You may imagine there were no union hours at this business, and the officers and men were kept busy standing by guns throughout the daylight hours and disguising the vessel at night for turning round before daybreak. The First Lieutenant's hours were some 24 hours per day with an addition for longitude when steaming West!

On this particular voyage, June 1st to 7th, as far as I remember, we were in touch with enemy submarines each day, and sighted several torpedoed ships. One afternoon we steamed parallel with a German submarine some three miles to starboard of us for two hours, which, however, made no attack, and our Commander was too old a hand at the business to try to force an action which could only be unsuccessful.

On another morning, at 8am., we came up to what turned out to be the floating wreckage from the Turret Steamer *Clan Murray*, finding her crew or what was left of them, floating about on large wooden cases and debris. I was sent away in the port lifeboat to pick up the survivors, but on getting up on to the boxes found, on most of them, dead Lascars (oriental sailors) who had been unable to withstand the exposure. One white man whom I had noticed standing on a box some distance away swam over to the boat while I was examining a bunch of Lascars huddled on a box and picking out the live from the dead. After we pulled him into the boat he told me that he was the Second Engineer of the *Clan Murray*, which had turned over and sunk immediately she was torpedoed at 4am. that morning, and that the submarine had made three attempts to make him prisoner, but being a good swimmer he had evaded them by swimming and diving around his box until they left him alone. As the *Clan Murray* was about 150 miles from the Irish Coast, and he must have known that no W/T (wireless transmission) would have been sent out of the disaster, owing to her immediate sinking, the choice of being taken prisoner or standing on a box with about two inches of freeboard in the Atlantic, wet through, and dressed in a singlet and pair of pants, with no particular expectation of rescue, would not seem to have been a difficult one; however, he took the long chance and, as he well deserved, he won through, none the worse, I hope, for his adventure. I have forgotten the gentleman's name, and have never seen him since, but should be proud to take my hat off to him any time.

Only a total of eleven were found to be alive and picked up, and shortly afterwards transferred to an American destroyer, the dead being buried at once. At sea our Commander was on his *qui vive* and saw that the crew and armament was kept in the highest state of efficiency; he lived only to find and bring the enemy to action, and to be sure no mistakes would be made when he got him there.

Some of the crew of the Q-ship 'Pargust.'
Gus is in the front row, second right, wearing the rather unusual hat.

The morning of June 7th opened with a S.W. weather, haze and rain, and a fairly rough sea, an unlikely day to be attacked owing to the low visibility. However, at 8am, our alarm sounded to be followed immediately by the explosion of a torpedo on the starboard side of the engine room, killing the fireman on duty, but by some freak of circumstance allowing the engineer on watch, who was in the starboard engine room store and, therefore in the track of the explosion, to be picked up unconscious, but otherwise unhurt, floating on top of the engine room which was, of course, full of water, as was also No. 4 hold. The ship however floated almost upright, and except for the sluggish feel a ship has with a lot of loose water in her, was suiting the purpose nicely; all our disguises held in spite of the explosion, and now the abandon ship party got busy leaving the ship with all the appearance of panic. (Abandon ship was completed by 8.15).

The starboard lifeboat had been blown to matchwood by the torpedo and disappeared, and the after tackle of the small boat on the starboard side had been let go with a run, leaving the boat hanging on the end to assist in the deception. Lieut. Hereford, R.N.R., went away in charge of the abandon ship party of some 24 men in the two port boats, his instructions being to endeavour to lure the Submarine as near the *Pargust* as possible. Some minutes after the abandon ship party had left the ship the Submarine was seen to come to the surface ahead of us some 300 yards away, and shortly afterwards submerged, and with the periscope well out of the water, steamed slowly down our port side in the direction of the boats which were lying off the port quarter. Hereford then rowed his boats round to the starboard quarter, and the Submarine, after some minutes, came again to the surface right aft. After apparently scanning the ship closely from a distance of 100 yards or so from our stern, she steamed slowly up toward the boats which were now lying close under the starboard quarter, and were moving along towards our starboard beam.

In addition to an officer in the conning tower who was examining our ship closely through a pair of glasses, a second German had come up through a deck hatch with a rifle and was shouting to our boats to come alongside the Submarine. Hereford and his boat's crew now put up a splendid piece of bluff, backing and pulling on the oars in the rough sea as if trying to carry out the German's wishes, but all the time bringing the Submarine further along our starboard side and a matter of 50 yards away from it. The hunter was by now fast becoming the hunted.

When the Submarine had come into a position some two points abaft the beam the officer in her conning tower, still examining the ship intently with his glasses, suddenly stiffened his arms. The movement was his death warrant; Campbell watching him like a hawk from his hiding place on the bridge, saw this action, rang the firegong, and in three or four seconds our starboard broadside of four guns was pouring in shells at a target which was so close that it would be nearly impossible to miss. During the next minute the Submarine must have been struck by at least 40-50 twelve-pounder and four inch shells, to say nothing of machine gun and rifle fire; and it was very astonishing to see the amount of punishment these craft could take before being put completely out of action. (The bombardment began at 8.36, lasting four minutes).

The Submarine had no more than steerage way when fire was opened, but sailed slowly along our side and under our starboard bow and passed over to the port side, clearing our stern by only a few feet and being blanketed from our fire by our own bows for some little time. When she opened out again on the port side some 20 of her crew were standing on the deck waving their arms and our Commander had the cease fire gong sounded. After a few seconds, however, she was seen to be increasing speed, and no doubt would have got away from us on the surface into the haze, as we could not move; and Campbell had no alternative but to open fire again which was done. After a few rounds, more of her crew appeared on deck and she commenced to go down quickly by the stern, those of her crew who had not been killed by our fire jumping overboard as she sank, stern high in the air with a man astride of it, when an explosion in the fore end of her, finished her activities for all time.

Our boats rowed over to the position where she sank, but owing to the sea and swell, only reached the position with difficulty and managed to pick up two survivors, one of whom turned out to be an officer, the other an engine room rating. They were given medical attention, fed and clothed; and I am still waiting for the suit of clothes I gave to the rescued officer who was, at the time, most insistent in his assurance of recompensing me for same. Some few hours after the action we were taken in tow by a sloop and towed back to Queenstown, thence to Devonport for repair, all of which was uneventful; and the *Pargust* was in course of time repaired and sailed the seas under other names. (HMS *Crocus* took *Pargust* in tow at 12.30. Under escort from USS *Cushing* and HMS *Zinnia* they arrived back in Queenstown at 15.00).

At this stage of the war it was estimated that the destruction of a German Submarine saved this country some five million pounds, as that was the average amount of damage caused by each of the enemy's underwater craft; and the Admiralty about this time, probably at the instance of their chief humorist, decreed that the sum of 30s. given to the men serving in the Mystery Ships for fitting themselves out with clothing suitable for a Merchant Seaman -as, of course, no uniform could be worn - should be increased to two pounds!"

In the spring of 1930, shortly after the publication of Gus' account of the Pargust action, he sent a copy to his old boss, Admiral Bayly, who wrote to express his thanks saying:

> " It was most kind of you to send it, as it reminded me of the brave old
> days and the numerous brave people I was associated with."

OTHER SOURCES.

Other sources add a little more to Gus' account of the battle between the mine laying submarine, UC 29, and the *Pargust*. During the time in which the ship was being fitted out for its role as a Q-ship, Gordon Campbell asked for a defensive gun to be mounted on deck. By this stage of the war it had become commonplace for merchant vessels to carry such a gun and to go to sea without one would have attracted suspicion. When his request fell on deaf ears he decided to take matters into his own hands, having the dockyard make him a dummy gun of wood with a brass handle which his crew thought very amusing. During their time at sea the crew pretended to polish, clean and load what was basically a block of wood!

It is clear that Gordon Campbell was not happy about the shipwrecked merchantmen being aboard his ship but decided to make the best of it by revealing the true nature of the ship to the two officers who had survived and giving them instructions of what they should do in the event of a U-boat attack. As for the Lascars, he concluded that these cold, shivering, frightened men would make the ideal panic party without the need for training! Fortunately they were spared any further trauma by the arrival of the American destroyer.

Campbell's report reveals why Gus lost his spare set of clothes to a German officer, who was wet through, covered in oil and wounded. Leutnant zur See Hans Bruhn collapsed and was violently sick as soon as he was brought to the Captain's cabin, managing to compose himself enough to say, "Sir I am a naval officer and will not speak." Campbell's reply was that he was a very brave man and would be given a hot drink and change of clothes; this is where Gus came in! During the early stages of the action, Hans Bruhn and two other men had been ordered on deck to man one of the U-boat's guns but the high wind and heavy sea had washed them overboard before they could reach their post. They were in the sea by the time the *Pargust* began her bombardment. The only other survivor told Campbell that they had been at sea for many days and, although they had already sunk a number of French and Norwegian ships, they wanted to 'sink a Britisher' before they went home.

UC 29 had left Brunsbuttel on May 25th with a crew of thirty-one and armed with a 22-pound gun, a machine gun, three torpedoes and eighteen mines. They had followed their usual method of operation: laying their mines in groups of three and then hunting for merchant vessels. By the time UC 29 encountered the *Pargust*, her captain had just one torpedo left, having fired one at a destroyer and using the other to sink a sailing ship.

Whilst he was waiting to be towed back to port, Commander Campbell sent a wire to Admiral Bayly informing him of the action. The Admiral replied;

> "C.-in-C. to *Pargust*. I congratulate you and your crew most heartily on
> your magnificent record, and deeply regret the loss of one of your
> splendid ship's company."

The man who lost his life when the torpedo struck the ship, 27 year old Petty Officer Stoker K/932 Isaac Radford R.N, is commemorated on the Plymouth Naval Memorial.

NAVAL HISTORY IS MADE.

The crew of HMS *Pargust* were the first ship's company to be awarded the VC under Rule 13 of the Statutes of the Victoria Cross. This rarely used statute was invoked because whilst the gallantry and courage of the men of the *Pargust* was fully deserving of their nation's highest honour, it was not possible to distinguish any one man's conduct from that of another. Under such circumstances the rules allow for a ballot amongst officers and men to elect one man amongst each to be honoured.

Gordon Campbell himself would have made history as the first naval officer to be awarded a bar to his VC if he had accepted the result of the ballot of *Pargust's* officers which selected him as the officer recipient. Only one other man, Captain Noel G. Chavasse RAMC, won a VC and bar during the Great War, the bar being awarded posthumously. A bar to a medal is awarded when an individual has already earned that medal but performs an act which would render him eligible to receive it again. Noel Chavasse was the son of the Bishop of Liverpool, the man who had confirmed Gus into the church in 1900 when he was a young cadet on *Conway*.

Lieutenant Ronald N. Stuart DSO RNR: the officer elected VC on 'Pargust.' (Courtesy of Neil Clark).

The crew of the 'Pargust' chose Seaman William Williams DSM to receive the VC. (via Stephen Snelling).

The very nature of the work of the Q-ships meant that any one of the men on board 'could spoil the show' and, as Campbell felt that his original VC had been earned by the whole crew and not by any exceptional bravery on his behalf, he declined his officers' request that he accept a bar to his VC and was instead awarded a bar to his DSO and promoted to Captain. He was just 31 years old.

The second ballot of officers selected Campbell's second in command, thirty year old Lieutenant Ronald N. Stuart DSO RNR, to receive the VC. Like Gus, Ronald Stuart had travelled all over the world and had several narrow escapes during his twelve years as a merchant seaman. Researcher Neil Clark describes Stuart as a complex man who detested pomp and snobbery; someone who was hard on himself and who never understood why he had been awarded the VC, saying that his award was a tribute to all of the men of the *Pargust* not just to himself. He subsequently left to command his own Q-sloop and was to receive further honours in October 1917 when he helped to rescue a torpedoed American destroyer, the USS *Cassin*.

A ballot amongst the ratings awarded the second VC to twenty-six year old Seaman William Williams DSM RNR. Williams, the son of an Anglesey fisherman who had served on board Campbell's Q-ships since the autumn of 1915, was described by author Stephen Snelling as being a hard-working and thoroughly reliable seaman; one of the bravest men in an exceptionally brave ship's company. When *Pargust* was torpedoed at 8.00 the force of the explosion had freed the weights holding the gun covers in place. A moment of quick-thinking by William Williams was followed by thirty-six minutes of almost unimaginable strength and determination as he took the whole weight of the gun covers on himself until his captain seized his opportunity to open fire.

A total of sixteen medals were awarded to the officers and men of the *Pargust*, including the DSO for Lieutenant Hereford who had been in command of the panic party. Gus had been in charge of two of the guns which had caused the very swift demise of UC 29 and, as a result, the following announcement appeared in the '*London Gazette*' on 20th July 1917.

> "Honours for Services in Action with Enemy Submarines.
> The King has been graciously pleased to approve the award of the
> following honours, decorations and medals to Officers and men for
> services in action with enemy submarines; To receive the
> Distinguished Service Cross, Lieut. Charles George Bonner RNR."

The DSC was instituted in 1901 as a reward for Warrant and Subordinate Officers of the Navy, although at that time it was known as the Conspicuous Gallantry Cross. In 1914 the rules on eligibility were changed, meaning that anyone below the rank of Lieutenant-Commander could receive it. It is a plain silver cross with rounded edges having the royal cypher 'GVR' in the centre and a ribbon with equal stripes, two of navy and one of white. Approximately 1,800 DSC's were awarded during the Great War and lists of recipients were published in the '*London Gazette*'.

Two of the official documents which make reference to Gus' service on HMS *Pargust* contain items of particular interest. His officer papers have an entry which reads:

> Serving on HMS *Pargust* on 7-6-1917 when the ship was awarded VC
> for the destruction of an enemy submarine.

This was included on the records of all the men who took part in the ballot and the wording of it, that is to say the ship being awarded the VC, stands as a testament to their collective bravery. Another entry in the same papers reads:

> For service in action with enemy submarine high commendation conferred.
> Awarded DSC Gazette 20-7-17.

Two other items of interest are contained in his RNR officer training book. Both refer to a payment from the Naval Prize Fund. The first reads:

> May 20. Paid Prize Bounty for destruction of Schuau U.C. 29. 7-6-17.

The second entry shows that Gus received a total of £75 from the naval prize fund during his Q-ship career. The fund rewarded ship's companies for the capture or destruction of enemy vessels and was calculated by a shares system, with varying numbers of shares in the 'prize' being given to those of different ranks. The total award from the fund to the officers and men of HMS *Pargust* was £1,000.

TILL DEATH US DO PART.

After a very eventful few months Gus came home - to get married! On Friday 15th June he sent a telegram to Cissy, telling her that he would be home on leave on Saturday and that she was to arrange the wedding for the following Wednesday. Jane Bonner described the bride and groom in a letter to her daughters. She wrote:

> "Cissy wore a coat and skirt of shantung very well; ready-made hat
> to match, and dainty shoes and stockings. I never saw Cis look so

nice and her face quite soft and sweet. Gus looked handsome and
grand and held himself like a God, and was not awkward or nervous."

The ceremony took place at St Matthews Church, Walsall at 10.00 on 20th June 1917, Gus having chosen one of his fellow officers, Engineer-Lieutenant Leonard Loveless DSO DSC RNR, as his best man. The vicar waited as long as he possibly could in the hope that Lieutenant Loveless would arrive but he had been unable to get leave. His hastily drafted-in replacement was himself replaced when Cissy's brother Harold turned up at the very last minute to perform the role of Gus' best man.

Gus and Cissy on their wedding day, 20th June 1917, a day which Gus described as 'perfect.'

After the ceremony a party of sixteen went back to 'Minstead,' the Partridge family home, for a wedding breakfast of, "salmon, chicken, ham, sweets, strawberries and champagne galore." Amongst the many telegrams congratulating the newly-weds, were several from his fellow officers. Gordon Campbell, busy preparing for his next Q-ship simply wrote, "Hearty congratulations and best wishes. Campbell," and

Lieutenant Hereford added a postscript to his telegram saying, " I hear your bag is packed."

One telegram with a nautical theme said, "may your joys be as deep as the ocean and your troubles as light as the spray," whilst Asst. Paymaster Nunn wrote - rather amusingly considering what they had just been through together - that he hoped that Gus would survive the ceremony!

Jane Bonner was clearly impressed by the number of good wishes which her son had received from his fellow officers and by the gift which they sent to him. She wrote:

> "The postman brought a box for Gus and in it was a lovely silver
> rose bowl inscribed, 'To Lieutenant C.G. Bonner R.N.R. from
> Captain and Officers, HMS *Pargust*, on the occasion of his marriage
> June 1917.' Really, sailors are generous and open-hearted. He has
> only been with them two months and it is easily worth £15. A real
> beauty. Gus' speech made us laugh. He got up and said, 'my wife
> and I thank everybody for their kindness, particularly Mrs P'
> (his mother-in-law). Then he bit his lip, thought very deeply and
> said, 'well I think I have nothing more to say' and sat down. The
> vicar was amused."

Photographs were taken in the garden, before the happy couple left at 13.00 for a short honeymoon in the Lake District, describing their day as perfect. They returned to spend a few days at home before Gus had to report to Devonport at the end of June.

For almost two precious weeks he had been living a 'normal' life, and one wonders what was going through his mind as he left his young bride and the comparative peace and tranquillity of Aldridge to board the train for Devonport.

Chapter 5

DUNRAVEN:
HEROES ON THE BURNING DECK

Following the action with UC 29, *Pargust* was taken back to Devonport for repair but it soon became clear that the damage was much more extensive than first thought. Although she could and would be repaired, it was decided that Gordon Campbell should look for another ship. He chose the collier *Dunraven* which, at just over 3,000 tons, was slightly bigger than her predecessor having a double well deck and much larger poop. She had been built in Newcastle in 1910 and during her re-fit as a Q-ship she acquired the following:

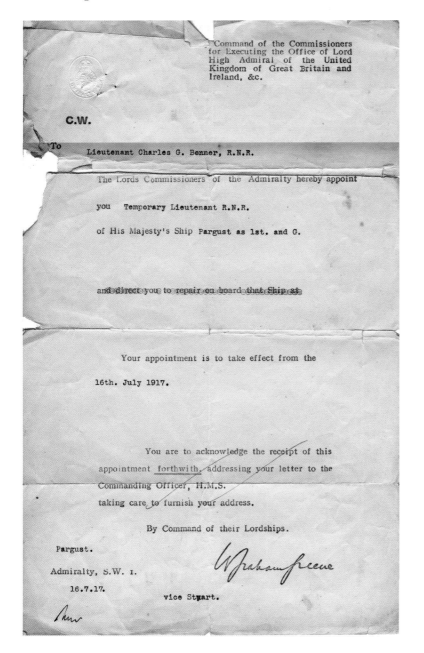

Command of the Commissioners
for Executing the Office of Lord
High Admiral of the United
Kingdom of Great Britain and
Ireland, &c.

C.W.

To   Lieutenant Charles G. Bonner, R.N.R.

The Lords Commissioners of the Admiralty hereby appoint

you   Temporary Lieutenant R.N.R.

of His Majesty's Ship Pargust as 1st. and G.

and direct you to repair on board that Ship as

Your appointment is to take effect from the

16th. July 1917.

You are to acknowledge the receipt of this
appointment forthwith, addressing your letter to the
Commanding Officer, H.M.S.
taking care to furnish your address.

By Command of their Lordships.

Pargust.

Admiralty, S.W. 1.

16.7.17.   vice Stuart.

A letter appointing Gus to the position of 1st Officer on HMS 'Pargust' in place of Ronald Stuart. It soon became clear that the ship would take too long to repair and so both officers and men were transferred to HMS 'Dunraven.'

53

A four inch gun which was positioned on the poop.

Two twelve-pounders sited in specially constructed 'houses' on either side of the ship on top of existing cabins. These 'houses' had no hinges but were kept in place by a weight which, when moved, would allow the whole of the 'house' to fall down.

Two tilting twelve- pounders sited on the forecastle and after-end.

Two 14 inch torpedo tubes.

Two depth charges.

Instead of the wooden 'dummy' gun which had been used on the *Pargust*, the *Dunraven* had a real two and a half pound defensive gun; but the crew, having grown quite fond of their wooden gun, kept it on the mess-deck of their new ship as a source of amusement.

Dunraven had three 'innovations' which were to prove crucial in the action to come, saving the lives of several men including Gus and Gordon Campbell. The captain of the Q-Sloop HMS *Heather* had recently been killed when a splinter of wood penetrated his look-out and imbedded itself in his head, so Campbell arranged for the bridge to be fitted with armour plating on three of its sides. Four collapsible railway trucks made of wood and canvas were taken on board; firstly as a means of disguising the ship - one day they would be clearly visible and the next day dismantled and laid on the deck to look just like planks of wood covered with canvas sheeting - and secondly to act as bait for a U-Boat commander who might presume that they were bound for the front line: making him especially keen to destroy them. The third innovation was a pipe, perforated with tiny holes, which was rigged to emit steam over the engine-room, thereby inducing the captain of a U-boat to believe that he had dealt a devastating blow to the ship.

The crew of the *Dunraven*, thought to have numbered about eighty, was much the same as the *Pargust* with one notable exception: following the departure of Ronald Stuart VC to captain his own Q-sloop, Gus was promoted to first officer. When Gus and Gordon Campbell first met, Campbell had said that he saw something in Gus which made him 'cut out' for Q-ship work. The award of Gus' DSC and his rapid promotion to first officer would seem to suggest that his captain's instincts were correct.

DUNRAVEN SETS SAIL.

Cissy was able to spend a few days in Devonport with her husband before the *Dunraven* left Plymouth on August 4th 1917, setting a course for Gibraltar after receiving reports of an enemy submarine in the Bay of Biscay whose commander preferred to use his gun at distance rather than utilise his torpedoes. This method of attack did not suit the *Dunraven* but, as it was now becoming common for U-boats to be fitted with big guns, it was something which had been discussed at length whilst they were in port and plans had been made for such an eventuality. The key to the operation was to use every conceivable method to induce the submarine to close in on the ship; in other words to convince the U-boat captain that their heavily armed decoy was a simple merchant ship, abandoned by her crew at the first sign of trouble. Gordon Campbell made it quite clear to his crew that he would not open fire until the enemy was within 1,000 yards, unless of course their cover was blown.

Consider for a moment the role of a Q-ship captain. His principal aim was to successfully engage a U-boat and destroy it. The safety of his men and the preservation of his ship was of secondary consideration; this is the nature of war. His ship was overcrowded with men in a permanent state of tension but discipline both above and below deck had to be strictly maintained in order for them to have any chance of achieving their principal aim and living to tell the tale. The captain had to create an atmosphere in which each man was absolutely clear of the role they were expected to play, whilst having total confidence in him to recognise his opportunity to open fire. No one could train or plan for the series of events which was about to unfold on *Dunraven*, anymore than anyone could have planned for William Williams to hold the gun covers in place on *Pargust*. Seaman Williams saw what needed to be done and did it, trusting in his captain to decide when his ordeal could come to an end and the gun covers be released. It would appear that Gordon Campbell was a man who had earned the trust and loyalty of his men.

THE ACTION BEGINS.

On the night of August 7th *Dunraven* received reports that the gun-firing submarine was in her vicinity. Campbell set a homeward course to meet her and the scene was set for one of the most famous of all Q-ship encounters. During the night the railway trucks were collapsed and laid on the deck; a move which was to prove significant for Gus and his gun-crew. At 10.58 the following morning, approximately 130 miles west of Ushant, the U-boat was sighted on the horizon heading straight for the ship, remaining in sight until 11.17 when she submerged. This gave the crew hope that the attack might come from a torpedo but the wireless reports about her favoured method of operation proved to be correct and at 11.43 she surfaced on the starboard quarter at approximately 5,000 yards distant and opened fire.

Gus was in charge of the four inch gun and its crew of eight men which was situated on the poop, on top of the magazine and close to the depth charges. The level of the poop was sunken to hide some of the gun, and a hatch built on top to hide more of it. The very top part of the gun was hidden by a derrick hung with either pieces of old canvas or washing. When the order was given to open fire, the hatch was designed to fall outward under its own weight, this in turn causing the rails around the poop to collapse inwards and the shrouds to fall towards the main mast. The whole system had to be robust enough to withstand an explosion without collapsing and also had to be immaculately maintained. Something as small as a piece of grit could prevent its use, which could, in turn, result in the loss of the ship and all on board.

In order to operate the gun, the crew had to crawl into the hatch from underneath via a trap-door. Gus was concealed within what looked like an ordinary hawser reel, a round drum on which ropes were reeled, which was sited between the defensive gun and the four-inch gun. In reality the dummy reel had slits cut in it and was fitted with a small periscope which enabled Gus to watch, relay information back to his captain and instruct his gun crew.

Gus and all of the concealed men watched and waited as the first scene of the well rehearsed drama unfolded. As befitting the crew of a merchant vessel, three men manned the defensive gun and returned fire, making sure that their shots fell well short, thereby encouraging the enemy to believe that he had the advantage of range and close in. Leading Seaman Cooper and Wireless Operator Statham would later receive the DSM, and Seaman William Williams VC a bar to his DSM, for their work in manning the gun whilst fully exposed to enemy fire. Their adversary was UC 71 under the command of Oberleutnant zur See Reinhold Saltzwedel, one of Germany's most popular and successful U-Boat commanders, who would destroy more than a hundred vessels in his two years at sea.

Campbell ordered a slight reduction in speed and sent fake wireless signals asking for help: deliberately not attaching any position to them. A signal had to be sent, otherwise the U-boat commander would have become suspicious, with the reduction in speed having to be carefully judged for the same reason. Although the submarine was too far away to know it, its guns were consistently missing their target: the *Dunraven* having slowed causing the shots to fall off the bow.

At 12.10, UC 71 ceased firing and closed on the *Dunraven*, stopping at 12.25 to re-open fire. At 12.40 a much more accurate shot fell just aside the engine-room and it was at this point that the first of the Q-ship's three innovations became useful: the perforated pipe emitting steam and thereby simulating a direct hit.

Dunraven came to a halt and the order was given to abandon ship. As the panic party made ready to leave, the helm was put to starboard bringing the port beam towards the submarine thus enabling Saltzwedel to see the crew leaving the seemingly ailing vessel. However, he continued to fire and his next shots dealt a devastating blow to the *Dunraven* and particularly to the crew of the four inch gun.

The first explosion blew Gus out of his dummy hawser reel and caused serious injury to Seaman Alex. S. Morrison and Wireless Operator Statham, several others sustaining relatively minor injuries. Seaman Morrison DSM RNR. was found by one of the abandon ship party but despite his dreadful injuries he was determined to get back to his post saying, "I am in charge of the depth charges and must get back to them." 25 year old Alex Morrison exemplifies the attitude of the men of the Q-ships. Campbell had often said that any one man could 'spoil the show' and Alex Morrison was determined that it would not be him. He would later be awarded the Conspicuous Gallantry Medal for his bravery but, sadly, Alex eventually succumbed to the injuries which he sustained during the action: Commonwealth War Graves records show that he died on the 19th September 1917 and was buried at Rake Lane Cemetery, Wallasey.

Such was the force of the explosion, subsequently found to have been caused by one of *Dunraven's* own depth charges, Campbell believed the magazine had been blown up and that the enemy would quickly realise the true nature of the ship. He took the decision to wire for assistance but rescinded it when he realised that the poop was still intact. Gus had been rendered temporarily unconscious by the first explosion which had blown him out of his hiding place. Rear-Admiral Sims said:

> "The first (shell) exploded a depth charge, 300 pounds of high-explosive
> which blew one of the officers out of the after control station where he
> lay concealed and landed him on the deck several yards distance. Here
> he remained a few moments unconscious; then his associates saw him,
> wounded as he was, creeping inch by inch back into his control position.

The hawser reel, within which Gus had been concealed, was destroyed in the explosion and so he crawled to his gun crew's position on the poop. The next two shells hit the poop setting it on fire and, unbeknown to Campbell, cutting communications with the bridge.

HEROES ON THE BURNING DECK.

The conditions for Gus and his men on the burning poop-deck were dire: several were wounded, thick, black smoke filled their lungs, fire raged all around them and the heat was almost unbearable. Worst of all they were on top of the magazine, a mini-arsenal which would inevitably explode as soon as the flames reached it. Natural inclination would surely be to get out of the appalling conditions and imminent danger which they found themselves in but, to their eternal credit, they stayed at their post and did their duty, hoping against hope that their captain's chance to fire on the enemy might come before they were blown up. They stood on crates as their boots smoked from the heat of the red-hot deck and held boxes of cordite in their arms or on their knees in an attempt to stop them exploding. One man took off his shirt and tore it into pieces so that his comrades could put it across their mouths to prevent them choking. Rear-Admiral Sims later wrote, somewhat dramatically:

> "Never did Christian martyrs stretched upon a gridiron suffer with greater heroism."

Meanwhile on the bridge, Campbell faced what he called a 'great decision.' The smoke from the burning poop which was drifting across the water obscured his view of the submarine, meaning that if he did open fire he would probably cause the U-boat to submerge, saving Gus and his men but failing in his mission to sink the U-boat. He wrote:

"To cold-bloodedly leave the gun's crew to their fate seemed awful, and the names of each of them flashed through my mind, but our duty was to sink the submarine. By losing a few men we might save thousands not only of lives but of ships and tons of the nations requirements. I decided to wait - a decision I could not have come to had I not had the most implicit confidence in Bonner and his gun's crew: them in particular, but the whole crew left on board in general - as we all knew what the poop contained in the way of explosives, and perhaps the whole ship would be blown up."

Rear-Admiral Sims wrote of Gordon Campbell's dilemma:

"Those who are acquainted with the practical philosophy which directed operations in this war will readily foresee the choice which was now made. The business of mystery ships, as of all anti-submarine craft, was to sink the enemy. All other considerations amounted to nothing when this supreme object was involved. The lives of officers and men, precious as they were in ordinary circumstances, were to be immediately sacrificed if such a sacrifice would give an opportunity of destroying the submarine. It was, therefore, Captain Campbell's duty to wait for the underwater boat to sail slowly around his ship and appear in clear view on the starboard side, leaving his brave men at the stern exposed to the fire, every minute raging more fiercely, and to the likelihood of a terrific explosion. That he was able to make this decision, relying confidently upon the spirit of his crew and their loyal devotion to their leader, again illustrates the iron discipline which was maintained on the mystery ships. The first explosion had destroyed the voice tube by means of which Captain Campbell communicated with his gun crew. He therefore had to make his decision without keeping his men informed of the progress of events - information very helpful to men under such a strain."

As well as Gordon Campbell having faith in Gus and his men, they, like William Williams on *Pargust*, had faith in him. Even though communication with their captain had been lost, his men were clear about what needed to be done and did it.

Approximately ten to fifteen minutes after the explosion which had caused the fire on the poop, Campbell was within seconds of bringing three of his 12-pound guns to bear on UC 71 at a range of four hundred yards when, by a quite extraordinary stroke of bad luck, the long anticipated explosion rocked the *Dunraven*, blowing the gun crew and ammunition into the air. One man was blown into the sea and picked up by the abandon ship party, whilst Gus and all but one of his men were incredibly fortunate to have their fall broken by the wood and tarpaulin of the collapsed railway trucks; had they fallen on to the iron deck their injuries would have been much more severe and probably fatal. The gun landed on the well-deck and the shells which had surrounded it landed in various places all over the ship, although none exploded. Campbell opened fire on the alerted and now submerging submarine but caused no damage.

Despite the fact that he was burned, concussed and bleeding profusely from a serious head wound, Gus managed to crawl up the gangway to the bridge and apologise to his Captain for leaving his post saying:

"I am sorry Sir to leave the gun without permission, but I believe I was blown up."

A FIGHT TO THE LAST.

One might have imagined that with his cover blown and his ship on fire, Campbell may have 'called it a day' but he had yet another trick up his sleeve. Gus and the ship's doctor, Surgeon Probationer Fowler, a young Scotsman who would later be awarded the DSC for his work on *Dunraven*, took the wounded below deck, while the remaining crew fought the wall of flame on the poop-deck. Gus had recovered from his initial concussion and, after his own wounds were attended to, he did what he could to care for his wounded men.

It is not clear as to where or when this photograph of Gus was taken but, given his head bandages and walking stick, it is likely to have been taken shortly after the action on 'Dunraven'.

Campbell knew that the Germans despised Q-ships, and considered the great propaganda coup should Saltzwedel have the opportunity of killing or capturing him, one of Britain's most famous Q-ship captains. Whilst his report suggests that leaving the scene would have been a much wiser course of action, he gave it barely a moment's thought saying:

"It savoured of running away."

At 13.20, UC 71 fired its torpedo from a distance of about 1,000 yards and it struck the engine room, blowing the railway trucks into the air and causing the bulkhead between the hold and the engine room to collapse. As the sea came rushing in, the order 'Q - Abandon Ship' was given and a second panic-party left the stricken ship. Two gun-crews, two torpedo operators, four on the bridge, the doctor tending his nine wounded men, and two others were all that were left on board; a total of thirty-four men of whom twenty-three were fit to fight. Once again they assumed the pretence that they were an abandoned ship, whilst watching and waiting for a chance to attack but the conditions in which they found themselves were quite unlike anything which had gone before. The submarine was not visible for twenty minutes, during which time the boxes of cordite and shells which had been distributed all over the deck were exploding as the fire reached them. The sea was gradually flooding the ship and as the boilers went out so did any possibility of escape. At 13.40, UC 71's periscope was sighted and for fifty minutes she circled and observed the ship, coming to the surface at 14.30 in a position on which none of *Dunraven's* guns could bear. Then the bombardment from both shells and machine guns began, Gordon Campbell's report stating that both the ship and the lifeboats were fired on.

This certificate details the injuries Gus sustained during the action in which he won the Victoria Cross.

It is easy to write this story and make it sound as though it were an adventure in a 'Boy's Own' magazine but what is not so easy is to convey is what it was actually like to be on that ship. The only complete eye-witness account comes from Gordon Campbell in his book, 'My Mystery Ships,' but of course the experience of a captain - the man who is making the decisions - is quite different from those who are carrying out orders and have only partial knowledge of the situation. Consider for a moment the conditions for Gus and the other wounded men: they had been blown up (in Gus' case twice), burnt, injured, shown courage which would earn two of them the nation's highest awards for bravery, and now found themselves in the saloon of a ship which was both in danger of flooding and on fire. They did not know what was happening on deck, although they could hear the explosions and, during the twenty minute bombardment, a piece of wood came straight through the deck and into the saloon just above their heads. Campbell would later report that he found one of the wounded men drinking his own blood. Yet this was no 'Boys Own' adventure story. This is the story of a group of ordinary men who did everything which was asked of them and more in the service of their country and their captain.

Campbell spoke to his crew via the voice-pipe during the bombardment, urging them to remember the VC which had been given to the *Pargust*. Then came the moment when the lives of Gordon Campbell and Lieutenant Francis Hereford were saved by the third innovation which had been ordered during the re-fit of the ship. The armour-plating on the bridge was peppered with splinters and, although Hereford was wounded by one of them, Campbell believed that the armour-plating had saved both of their lives.

After twenty minutes the U-boat submerged and Campbell and Hereford fired one torpedo each, with Campbell claiming that he heard one of them make contact with the submarine. He then called for urgent assistance and decided that when the next torpedo attack came he would order yet another abandon ship, leaving just one gun-crew on board; but it was not to be. Saltzwedel had run out of both torpedoes and ammunition when, quite by chance, the USS *Noma*, Vincent Astor's private yacht loaned to the United States navy as a patrol vessel, arrived and fired at the U-boat which then left the scene.

Details from Saltzwedel's own report, sent to Gus after the war, shows that he only realised that he was dealing with a Q-ship at the end of the action. He reported seeing a steamer of the Blue Funnel Line at noon on August 8th and opening fire on her. He believed that he had scored two hits and that the steam, emitted from the perforated pipes to simulate a hit, was in fact real. He did not see the gun-crew blown into the air, nor was he aware that one man had been rescued by a lifeboat. He recorded ten hits after the second panic-party left and reported that he saw no signs of life as he steamed around the ship. Having run out of torpedoes and with the ship slowly sinking, he decided to 'sheer off' and see what happened. He records that a yacht and two destroyers arrived and that the crew of the ship returned to put the fires out. His report ends at 21.00 stating that darkness prevented further observation.

Reinhold Saltzwedel, who was awarded the Pour Le Merite (commonly known as the Blue Max) following the action with the *Dunraven*, was killed less than four months later when his U-boat hit a mine. Although minefields were a hazard for U-boats, knowledge of their location meant that a good commander could either avoid the area or negotiate a safe path through it. Reinhold Salzwedel was a good commander but, on this occasion, desperately unlucky. His U-boat, UB 81, is believed to have detonated a mine in an area in which there were no minefields, leading to speculation that a mine had broken free from another area and been carried by the tide. Reinhold Saltzwedel perished along with most of his crew. He had celebrated his 28th birthday just a week earlier.

THE END FOR DUNRAVEN.

The USS *Noma* came alongside the *Dunraven* at 16.00; four and a quarter hours had passed since the first shot had been fired. Destroyers HMS *Attack* and HMS *Christopher* arrived and quickly sent their medical staff on to the ailing ship to treat the injured men, two of whom were then transferred to the *Noma* which made full steam to Brest so that they could be treated. The fire was put out and some of the damage patched up by 18.45 as the *Christopher* took the ship in tow. Gordon Campbell went below to see the remaining wounded whose first question was, " have we got him Sir?" Campbell wrote:

HMS 'Attack' coming to the aid of the stricken 'Dunraven.'
(US Naval Historical Center).

" To my everlasting regret I had to tell them I hadn't. They said, 'we've
done our bit' and if ever men had, they had."

A message was sent to Admiral Bayly who replied:

"Hearty congratulations on your brave fight. Hope ship will be saved.
Very well done."

Towing the *Dunraven* proved to be slow and difficult but with little to be done to aid the operation, most
of the crew were able to get some much needed rest during the night and at daybreak on August 9th they
woke to find the situation unchanged: the ship only making a knot or two but in no immediate danger of
sinking. During the day the weather worsened and as darkness fell it was decided that all but twenty of the
crew would leave the ship. Although bandaged and quite clearly unfit for duty, Gus asked his captain to
be allowed to stay; a request which was granted and a chair was bought to the bridge for him to sit down
and witness the final hours of a ship which was to change his life forever. Both Campbell and others wrote
of Gus's influence on the crew, saying that his determination and bravery had a significant effect on them
and that his happy disposition cheered everyone up.

At 21.00, the job of towing the *Dunraven* was taken over by the tugs *Sun II* and *Atlanta*, but by this time more
than half of the ship was underwater. Clearly desperate not to lose her, Campbell waited another four and
a half hours before giving the order for the tugs to cast off the tow and for the remaining crew, who were
by now wading through water, to fall in. Gordon Campbell's description of the last moments of his ship
paints a vivid picture:

"I found the men fallen in, in deadly silence; it was a pitch dark night
and blowing very fresh. I now witnessed a sight, by no means
uncommon in the annals of the chivalry of the sea, but one which
would long live in my memory. The *Christopher* had closed and was
sending her whaler. I realised that with the heavy sea running it would

be unwise to put more than four men into her, and I also realised that she wouldn't do more than one trip, so I gave the order, 'Four men to get into the boat only.' Not a man moved: they all knew that there would be only one trip, and no one wanted to go before the other. I therefore had to name four to go. The water was now rising round us, and I ordered the remainder to fall in on the forecastle head. Still complete silence was maintained except for the wind and the sea."

However, Lieutenant Commander Peters of the *Christopher* was not giving up easily and, in a great feat of seamanship, managed to bump against the sinking ship and then fall away with the waves; each time Campbell called out the name of one man to jump in the darkness from the rapidly sinking *Dunraven* to the safety of the *Christopher*. Eventually there were no more names to be called and the Captain himself made the leap to safety. With an air of defiance and determination as strong as that of her crew, the *Dunraven* refused to be sunk by gunfire: the *Christopher* needing to use a depth charge to sink her. Gordon Campbell's report shows that HMS *Dunraven* finally disappeared beneath the waves at 3.17 on August 10th 1917.

Several years after the war had ended, Gordon Campbell received a four-page document from a German source, detailing the action from a German point of view, which he forwarded to Gus. Part of it read:

"One cannot but admire the endurance of the crew of the *Dunraven* in these circumstances nor deny soldierly recognition of their wait on the hot deck for the expected explosion.... It is true that the Q-ship captain, who already claimed to have sunk four submarines, in this case met his match, but it must be confessed that the submarine, in spite of all its care, was several times saved by its greater luck."

BACK ON DRY LAND.

Gus was taken to hospital to be treated for his injuries and a telegram was sent to Cissy informing her that her husband had been wounded. Gordon Campbell spent what were to be his last few days as a Q-ship captain preparing reports and visiting Gus and the other wounded men in hospital. Admiral Bayly told him that his service on Q-ships had come to an end and, whilst Campbell demanded to be allowed to continue, Bayly was adamant. Rear-Admiral Sims sent a letter to Campbell suggesting that the Allies could not risk the loss of morale which would result from his death and that whatever his natural inclination, his skills should now be utilised in a different way.

Speaking during a lecture tour, many years after the war had ended, Gordon Campbell said of the men with whom he had served:

"No more credit was due to me than to any other man on my ship. No man could have done more than each of them did. They were a magnificent lot of fellows."

Naval rules prevented the officers of the *Dunraven* from presenting their captain with a token of their appreciation and so they sent a gift of a silver salver to Mrs Campbell, who in turn wrote to Gus thanking him and his fellow officers for their generosity.

By the end of August Gus had left hospital and was fit enough to attend the final parade service for the crew of the *Dunraven* at the church of the Devonport Naval Barracks.

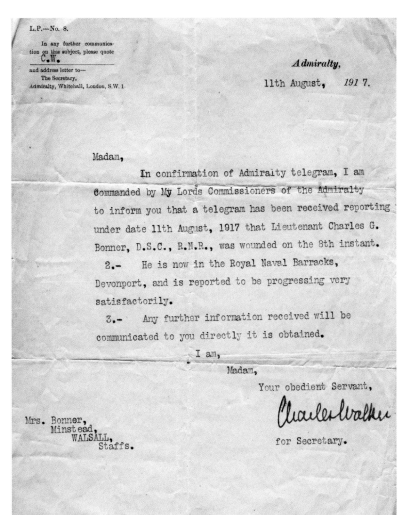

L.P.—No. 8.

In any further communication on this subject, please quote

C.W.

and address letter to—
The Secretary,
Admiralty, Whitehall, London, S.W. 1

Admiralty,

11th August, 191 7.

Madam,

In confirmation of Admiralty telegram, I am Commanded by My Lords Commissioners of the Admiralty to inform you that a telegram has been received reporting under date 11th August, 1917 that Lieutenant Charles G. Bonner, D.S.C., R.N.R., was wounded on the 8th instant.

2.- He is now in the Royal Naval Barracks, Devonport, and is reported to be progressing very satisfactorily.

3.- Any further information received will be communicated to you directly it is obtained.

I am,

Madam,

Your obedient Servant,

Charles Walker

for Secretary.

Mrs. Bonner,
Minstead,
WALSALL,
Staffs.

It must have come as a great relief to Cissy to know that her husband was making satisfactory progress.

For those who are interested in only the bare facts and statistics of war, the action between UC 71 and HMS *Dunraven* was a failure from the British point of view: the ship was sunk and the enemy escaped. But this 'failure' is widely acknowledged as one of the greatest encounters between a U-boat and a Q-ship, resulting in praise from all quarters, a payment of £300 from the prize fund (quite unusual considering that the U-boat had not been destroyed), and the award of more than forty medals to the officers and men. Amongst Gus Bonner's personal papers is a letter from Admiral Sims of the U.S. Navy. It reads:

" In my opinion the fight of the *Dunraven* is the finest of them all as a military operation and the most deserving of complete success. It is purely incidental that the submarine escaped. That was simply due to an unfortunate piece of bad luck... I know nothing finer in naval history than the conduct of the after-gun crew..."

The Admiralty wrote of their appreciation of the gallantry, skill and devotion to duty which had been displayed but the greatest praise came from the King himself who said:

"Greater bravery than was shown by all officers and men on this occasion could hardly be conceived."

Following a ballot amongst the crew of the after-gun, Petty Officer Ernest Pitcher DSM RN was awarded the Victoria Cross. Ernest, who had joined the Navy in 1903, had served on Q-ships since 1915, receiving his DSM for the action on *Pargust*. He received his VC at an investiture at Buckingham Palace in December 1917.

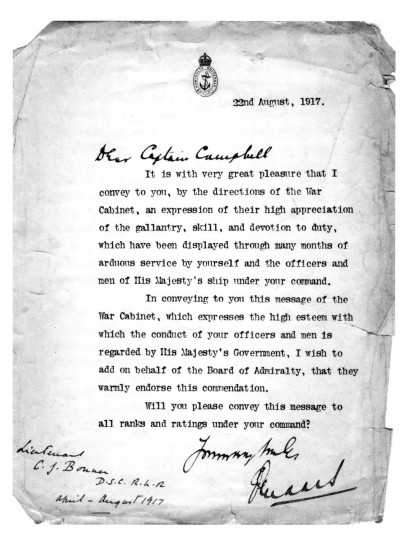

22nd August, 1917.

Dear Captain Campbell

It is with very great pleasure that I
convey to you, by the directions of the War
Cabinet, an expression of their high appreciation
of the gallantry, skill, and devotion to duty,
which have been displayed through many months of
arduous service by yourself and the officers and
men of His Majesty's ship under your command.

In conveying to you this message of the
War Cabinet, which expresses the high esteem with
which the conduct of your officers and men is
regarded by His Majesty's Government, I wish to
add on behalf of the Board of Admiralty, that they
warmly endorse this commendation.

Will you please convey this message to
all ranks and ratings under your command?

Gordon Campbell asked for this letter to be photographed and a copy sent to each man who had been involved in the action between HMS 'Dunraven' and UC 71.

Following his release from hospital, Gus wrote to his family to assure them that he was on the mend. Having had the privilege of reading many of Gus Bonner's letters, which are sometimes amusing and always have more regard for what is happening in everyone else's life rather than his own, it was a delight to read a letter which he sent to his parents at the time he had heard the first hint that he might be awarded the VC. He wrote on the top, "Everything in this letter is private and confidential." Far from his usual measured style of writing, this letter comes from a son who believes that he may soon receive his country's highest honour and desperately wants to share the news with his family. It is published in full here and contains what is probably one of the best lines in the book:

"By every law and regulation (I) was killed on three different occasions."

A few days later he got the leave he was hoping for and was able to come home to tell his parents what had happened on *Dunraven*. Jane Bonner, of course, wanted to share the story with her daughters but said that Gus had asked that nothing be put down on paper. Jane wrote:

"Do look out in the papers. You may see something very interesting.
The old chap (Gus) sat and told me the whole thing through last night.
It made my blood curdle. How he escaped is a miracle. He really has
been splendid and seems to think of nothing but Campbell and the boat
he is to have."

Every thing in this letter is *Private*
& Confidential.

12. 8. 17.

Dear Father & Mother

Thanks very much for your letter recd this afternoon am out of the Doctor's hands now except for a few dressings. had dozens of small wounds and burns but not one of any account and am quite well again now in fact have not been bad, Our Capt. has ~~been~~ gone to Queenstown till Wed. then we shall know all about things and how we stand for leave. I half believe I shall get the V.C. but please don't say anything

about it until it comes this time as it is not certain of course till the Admlty decide, I was quite the star turn in the fight, And by every law and regulation was killed on 3 different occasions, by shells and explosions, am feeling quite unkillable now, though I don't want another dose quite so bad as that again, for a day or two, Got a long letter from Doll seemed quite fit when she wrote, Hope to get home on Wed. or Thurs, but can't be too sure yet for a day or two it all depends on what our C in C at Queenstown wants us to do next, There will be a big surprise at the Admlty very soon, I hear Jellicoe is

getting chucked out and our Boss Adml. Bailey from Queenstown going in his place, very much hope it works as Campbell and our bunch are his particular pets and we shall all be sure of A.1. jobs with him on top. Also the British Navy won't be left to stagnate in harbour any longer. Well keep well and look after yourselves hope to see you in a few days

Very best love to all
I remain,
Ever your most loving Son
Gus

Gus' letter to his parents, in which he says that he 'half believes' he may be awarded the VC.

In September Jane wrote that both Gus and Gordon Campbell were spending a lot of time at the Admiralty; then came the news which they had been waiting for. Sam and Jane may well have taken out the carefully folded letter that Gus had written at Christmas 1913, in which he describes himself as a selfish pig and expresses a wish that his parents would live long enough for him to be able to repay them for their kindness and forbearance to him. Not only were they about to become local celebrities but the bravery of their second son, Charles George Bonner DSC RNR, was to ensure that the family name would be forever remembered in Aldridge and further afield. Within a few months this son of an Aldridge farmer would become Gus Bonner VC.

CChapter 6
VICTORIA CROSS

Prior to the inception of the Victoria Cross, only officers of the rank of major and above could expect to have their bravery honoured by their country: being awarded the junior Order of the Bath for acts of heroism. For the ordinary soldier or sailor the honour of serving their Sovereign and country and a modest wage was all they could expect, no matter what feat of valour they might accomplish. The Crimean War (1853-1856) was to change all that. For the first time a corps of war reporters brought the plight and heroism of ordinary British soldiers into the public eye, capturing their imagination as never before. The ground swell of opinion was that something needed to be done, not just to improve conditions but also to ensure that heroism was recognised no matter what the rank of the individual.

Prince Albert and Queen Victoria played significant roles in making the VC what it is today. It was Prince Albert who vetoed the Government's preferred title of Military Order of Victoria which he felt sounded too aristocratic and the Queen herself was involved in choosing the design, wisely rejecting the Government's chosen inscription, 'For The Brave', on the grounds that it might imply that non-recipients were not brave, preferring the words 'For Valour'.

The Victoria Cross was founded by Royal Warrant on 29th January 1856, being a Maltese cross of bronze, 1.375 inches wide with a suspender bar and v-shaped link. The face of the medal bears the royal crest, with an escroll underneath on which are written Victoria's chosen words: 'For Valour.' The date of the act of bravery is engraved in the centre of the circle on the reverse of the cross, with the recipient's details on the bar. Since 1918, all VCs have been issued with what the Imperial War Museum describes as, 'a wine red ribbon' but, as Gus's award preceded this date, his original ribbon was blue to indicate a naval recipient. However, after the war Gus and all other living naval Victoria Cross holders were asked to return their blue ribbons to be replaced by wine red ones.

The most prized of all medals: the Victoria Cross. (Original drawing courtesy of Kim J. Gargett.)

The medal was, and still is, made by Hancocks of Mayfair who, since 1906, have included a miniscule mark to deter would-be forgers of this most prized of all medals. The warrant of 1856 set fifteen rules and ordinances for the awarding of a VC which were to be, "inviolably observed and kept." These rules have seen a number of changes over the years and there are many excellent books on the subject. However the sixth rule bears inclusion in this brief history because it, above all others, sums up the unique nature of the award. It reads:

"It is ordained with a view to place all persons on a perfectly equal footing
in relation to eligibility for the Decoration, that neither rank, nor long service,
nor wounds, nor any other circumstance or condition whatsoever, save the merit
of conspicuous bravery shall be held to establish a sufficient claim to the honour."

NAVAL VCS.

Forty-two VCs were awarded for naval operations during the Great War (not including those awarded to naval men for actions in the air or on land), of which nine were men of the RNR and six of the RNVR. On 17th May 1918, the 'London Gazette' announced the award of a posthumous VC to another local man, Ordinary Seaman John Henry Carless RN, for conspicuous bravery and devotion to duty at Heligoland Bight on November 17th 1917. John Carless was fatally injured during the action on HMS *Caledon* but official reports and personal recollections tell of his extraordinary bravery: continuing to man his gun and encourage others around him until he finally collapsed and died at his post less than a week after his 21st birthday. A bronze bust of Seaman Carless VC RN stands outside Walsall's Central Library and the town has named two streets, Caledon Street and Carless Street, after one of its bravest sons.

A total of eight VCs were awarded to the men of the Q-ships. Five have already been mentioned in this book, namely Campbell, Stuart, Williams, Pitcher and, of course, Gus; the remaining three being, Lieutenant William Sanders, Skipper Thomas Crisp and Lieutenant Harold Auten.

Lieutenant William E. Sanders RNR won his VC on 30th April 1917 in an action which saw the men of the Q-ship HMS *Prize* withstand a twenty minute bombardment from a U-boat, take prisoners and guide their badly damaged ship back to safety. Although both Sanders and the U-boat captain (who was one of the prisoners) believed that the submarine had been sunk, somehow an amazing feat of seamanship by a young German officer resulted in not only the badly damaged U-boat getting home but also enabling a description of the *Prize* as a 'trap-ship' to be circulated amongst all submarine commanders. The award of the Victoria Cross to Lieutenant Sanders appeared in the 'London Gazette' on June 22nd 1917 and, although he knew of the honour which had been bestowed upon him, he did not live to receive it: the *Prize* being sunk and all hands lost during an encounter with a U-boat on 14th August 1917.

Thomas Crisp DSC RNR was skipper of the armed fishing vessel *Nelson* when, on the 15th August 1917, she was fired on by a submarine in the North Sea. One shell resulted in injuries which were all too familiar to those in the trenches: Thomas Crisp was partially disembowelled and had both legs severed whilst standing at the tiller. It is impossible to read the account of his bravery without wondering at the inner strength and courage shown by both himself and his eighteen year old son who was also onboard the *Nelson* and witnessed his father's terrible injuries and subsequent death. Somehow, despite the fact that he had been almost cut in half, Thomas Crisp was still conscious and when his son Thomas came to his aid he encouraged him to take the tiller; reassuring the rest of the crew and telling them to do their best. He ordered that a message be sent off by pigeon asking for assistance because the ship was sinking and that sensitive papers be thrown overboard. However, his final order to throw him overboard, was not carried out. One by one the crew abandoned the sinking ship, leaving just Thomas Crisp and his son on-board. Thomas Jnr kissed his father goodbye, although he believed that by this time he was already dead. Thomas Crisp's wife had died just two months earlier, so it fell to Thomas Jnr to receive his father's posthumous VC from the King on 19th December 1917, along with his own DSM awarded for the same action.

The final Q-ship VC of the Great War was awarded to Lieutenant Harold Auten DSC RNR. When HMS *Stock Force* was hit by a torpedo on July 30th 1918, the damage to both men and ship was devastating and yet, injured and in a state of shock, they continued with the well rehearsed plan. In the saloon the ship's doctor waded knee deep in water as he treated the badly injured; makeshift repairs and brute force being needed to stop the gun screens collapsing. For forty minutes Harold Auten waited for his chance to fire on the submarine, eventually managing to bring two guns to bear. Although he and most of the crew believed that the U-boat had been sunk, official records show no submarines lost on that day. The courage of the officers and men of the *Stock Force* earned them a number of medals including the VC for Auten himself.

CHARLES GEORGE BONNER VC.

In one of his final reports as a Q-ship captain, Gordon Campbell recommended that Gus be given command of his own ship and singled him out for particular praise for his conduct on the *Dunraven*. Many years later, Gordon Campbell dedicated one of his books to Gus whom he described as:

"The bravest man I ever met."

In a report dated 18th August 1917 he wrote:

"He displayed exceptional zeal and bravery in the face of the enemy."

He also wrote on Gus' official papers:

"Exceptionally brave, has no fear. Very capable. Suitable to command a small ship."

Both of Gordon Campbell's comments were acted upon: Gus was informed that he was to receive the Victoria Cross for his bravery in the face of the enemy and, a month after the action on *Dunraven*, he received a letter from the Admiralty appointing him to the auxiliary schooner, *Eilian*, which was at Devonport being fitted for her new role as Q-ship. He was told that he would take charge of the vessel upon commissioning and that, as before, he was to provide his own clothes. At the peak of the Q-ship campaign there had been thirteen Q-ships under the command of Admiral Sir Lewis Bayly at Queenstown but, by the end of 1917, this had been reduced to just three, of which *Eilian* was the smallest. Looking at the pictures of this elegant vessel, which had previously accommodated a merchant crew of just six men, it is difficult to see how she could ever expect to take on a U-boat and survive.

Gordon Campbell's carefully chosen words are likely to have played a significant role in the decision to award Gus the Victoria Cross.

Campbell had his own concerns about the *Eilian*. He was worried that his friend was about to go to sea again in what he called 'a dangerous looking ship' and decided to write to the Admiralty to ask whether it would be possible for Gus to receive his VC from the King before he left, no doubt fearing that he may not return; a fate which had already befallen a fellow Q-ship commander, William Sanders. Campbell's request resulted in a rather unusual and hurried royal presentation during the first weekend of October 1917. According to Gus' family, one of the consequences of this hurried investiture was that his VC had not been engraved when it was presented to him, and so Gus asked the King if he would be allowed to have it engraved; the King replying that he felt that such a course of action would be quite in order.

SANDRINGHAM.

Although the lives of Gordon Campbell and Gus Bonner would take quite different directions after the war, the few months they had served together on His Majesty's Q-ships had brought about a friendship which would last for the rest of their lives. Theirs was certainly a friendship borne out of mutual respect but it was also based on a shared sense of humour which is very evident in the following letter which Gus wrote to Gordon Campbell regarding his investiture.

"Dear Captain Campbell,

I have just returned from Sandringham after spending the week-end at York Cottage and being invested with the VC and, as I know you have been the chief cause of all this happening, I want to thank you right away and feel that perhaps you would like to hear all about it.

On Friday at 10p.m. I received a Naval Signal at my digs in Saltash ordering me to report to the Fourth Sea Lord at 10a.m. on Saturday. I had little time to spare and thinking an investiture was being held at Buckingham Palace, and that I would probably travel back to Devonport on Saturday night, took only a small dispatch bag and sword and proceeded by the midnight train.

I reported myself to the Fourth Sea Lord at 10 the following morning, and he told me I was to proceed to Sandringham by the next train and spend the weekend with the King. This rather staggered me, and I explained to him that I could not possibly go, having no clothes or luggage and no time to get any, but he said that was quite in order; I had to go anyhow, and that I should find everything O.K., and he finished up by saying he had really no idea of the procedure, as he had never been himself.

I was given a letter of introduction to Colonel Wigram and started off. At Kings Lynn, unfortunately, I upset part of my tea-basket over an elderly gentleman sitting opposite me, who was naturally very annoyed and did not hesitate to say so. At Wolferton Station I was met by two huge men in green liveries, one of whom seized my dispatch bag and sword, and the other was most anxious to empty the guard's van to get out my heavy luggage. I was then asked to step into the Royal Brougham (carriage) and was driven to Colonel Wigram's residence, where I was met by the Colonel and Mrs Wigram and also introduced to the only other guest, the Dean of Norwich.

At 6.p.m. the Dean and myself were driven to York Cottage, and Captain Fausset took me along to the King's study, where he left me with H.M. who was awfully nice. He gave me my VC, and asked me a lot about you, and settled down to tell me some of his own sea experiences until dinner-time. As I left his study I found the Queen and Princess Mary outside in the Hall, and was presented to them, and then ushered into a room where the Staff was waiting. The first one in the line was the old gentleman I had upset the tea over on the train. He was now in evening dress, smothered in orders and decorations, and he turned out to be Lord Marcus Beresford, the Master of the Horse. On seeing me, he used some expression which sounded like a smothered curse, but told me to stand next to him, as I needed someone to look after me, and during the rest of my visit was most charming to me whenever I met him.

At dinner I sat next to the King, and my opposite number, the Dean, next to the Queen. After the Queen, Princess Mary and the ladies had retired, I was turned over to the Duke of York, and later taken into the drawing-room to talk to the Queen. About eleven our car was reported alongside, and the Dean and myself were driven back to Colonel Wigram's house, where we spent about an hour in his study, and about midnight the Colonel asked me to ring up the War Office to ask for the latest reports, and then the Admiralty, and I must say I had no idea anyone in the Admiralty could be so polite and obsequious as the gentleman, whoever he was, who reported to me.

I got to bed shortly after midnight, and was called at 7.30 by my servant, who brought me a tray of tea and toast, inquired what time I would like my bath, and what temperature. The only temperature I could think of was 32 degrees Fahr., and that seemed rather cold. The servant returned at bath time with a towel about the size of a Turkey carpet over his arm and escorted me to the bathroom. After breakfast I walked about the grounds with the Dean.

Later I walked to church with H.M., and was put in the front pew with Sir Dighton Probyn V.C., he being the oldest and myself the youngest V.C. at the moment. After church the King asked me to walk over with him to see Queen Alexandra at Sandringham House. Queen Alexandra was most gracious, and patted me on the back, and I was asked to sign her autograph book. After that I walked back with H.M. to York Cottage, and after lunch, said good-bye to them all, and was motored up to Kings Lynn after a most enjoyable week-end, everyone from H.M. down doing their utmost to give me a good time, especially Colonel and Mrs Wigram, and I shall always have most happy recollections of my visit there.

I hope to see you again soon, and meantime remain,
Yours very sincerely,   C.G. Bonner."

Gus returned from Sandringham with this photograph of York Cottage,
several sheets of headed notepaper and, of course, his VC!

Referring to Gus' account of his visit to Sandringham, Gordon Campbell, writing in the *'Daily Sketch'* in 1933, said:

> "In spite of the humorous side of the yarn, I know Bonner felt that
> the King, by doing him such an honour, was expressing his high
> appreciation of the wonderful service of the officers of the R.N.R.
> during the Great War."

The Admiralty Citation for Gus' VC, not published until after the war, reads as follows:

Lieutenant Charles George Bonner DSC RNR

Awarded the Victoria Cross in recognition of his conspicuous gallantry and consummate coolness and skill, in action with an enemy submarine. This officer, after being blown out of his control station by the explosion of a depth charge due to shell fire, crawled back into the 4inch gun hatch with the gun's crew. They there remained at their posts with a fire raging in the poop below and the deck getting red hot, knowing all the time that they would be blown up as the secondary supply and magazine were immediately below. When the explosion took place, the gun was shifted bodily, and the gun's crew blown up in the air, one man being blown overboard, but fortunately none of them were killed, and only four wounded. Lieut. Bonner, although wounded himself, did what he could for two who were with him in the wardroom.

THE PRESS.

Letters from Sam and Jane Bonner to their daughters, Mary and Dolly, show how excited and proud they were of their son's achievements: Jane Bonner describing it as a fairytale. But, in the week following the investiture, Jane was much too busy to write to her daughters and so she arranged for Aunt Helen to make sure that the girls were kept up to date with all the news. Aunt Helen wrote her letter to Mary and Dolly in the form of a diary of events. On the 8th of October she wrote:

> "Up came your Nellie (Pa was breakfasting in bed) with your letters,
> and one from Cissie to say Gus had been sent for to Sandringham
> and that he was to have the VC on the Saturday. Great excitement.
> After a little time in she bursts again with my *'Daily Telegraph'* and
> bounces into Pa's room with the *'Daily Post'* where the Court Circular
> news was, 'Lieut. C G Bonner had the honour etc etc.' We nearly all
> had a fit, but didn't quite. Then when Pa came down he wrote on a
> piece of paper all the items of interest about Gus for when the
> reporters came."

Sam Bonner was very wise to write down everything he could about Gus. Within hours the first of what was to be a stream of newspaper reporters arrived, with each of them asking for both information and photographs of Gus. During the coming days, the Bonner family were to experience a taste of national fame and to find out just how insistent reporters could be!

On the morning of Monday October 8th 1917 three reporters came to Manor Farm, Aldridge along with a stream of visitors wishing to offer their congratulations. In her letter to Mary and Dolly, Aunt Helen said:

> "People came in to congratulate Ma and Pa. Poor Ma found tea
> making most trying."

After the Strafe

(With apologies to Southey)

I

It was a summer's evening,
Old Samuel's work was done,
And he before the farmhouse door
Was sitting in the sun;
And by his side his faithful wife
Sat knitting for her very life.

II

She saw her grandchild Michael-kin
Roll something large and round
Which he, whilst playing in the hall,
Upon the stand had found;
He came to ask what he had found
That was so long, and smooth, and round.

III

Old Samuel took it from the boy
Who stood expectant by;
And then the old man shook his head,
And heaved a natural sigh -
"It is a shell case, Mic," said he
"That fell in that Great Victory".

IV

"Now tell us what 'twas all about"?
Young Michael-kin he cries;
And Granny Jane looks up at him
With retrospective eyes;
"Now tell us all about the war,
And what they strafed each other for?

V

"It was the 'Q' boats". Samuel said,
"That put the 'Subs' to rout
"And to this day the Bosches they
"Could never make them out.
"And even Admiral Sims", quoth he,
"Wrote, "T'was a famous Victory."

VI

"They say it was a gory sight
"After the explosion past;
"And your brave Uncle Gus was found
"Unconscious by the mast:
"But things like this, you know, must be,
"Ere men attain to the V.C."

VII

"Great praise the Captain Campbell won,
"And your good Uncle Gus;
"And all the valiant men besides
"Who kept the foe from us:
"Ah! Ah! my little Mic" said he.
"It was a Famous Victory."

This poem is thought to have been written by Gus' father, Samuel.
'Little Mic' was Gus' nephew.

Aunt Helen describes the telegrams as 'pouring in' and, after a hectic day, they had just decided to take tea early at 16.15, when a knock was heard at the front door:

> "I went to the door. No one there, but a motor car by the front gate.
> Heard some one tramping into the kitchen, thought it must be Aunt
> Dora. Saw a strange, pompous, untidy, dirty man. 'Is Lieutenant
> Bonner VC here? I am from the *'Daily Sketch'*. Have only 10 minutes.
> Come down from London on purpose to photograph him.' Most
> indignant that he wasn't here. 'What not come home after such an
> honour as that conferred on him? What not a photo of him left? But
> I must have one, I have come all the way from London......"

Jane Bonner gave this rather rude man one of Gus and Cissy's wedding photographs and, after taking some shots of the house, he left. For the rest of the evening a constant stream of well-wishers continued to knock at the front door of Manor Farm, Aunt Helen describing the stream of visitors as incessant. The following day more reporters arrived, one of whom was a somewhat bad-tempered man from the *'Daily Mirror'* who began by saying:

> "Can I ask you first if the man from the *'Daily Sketch'* has been?"

When he was told that the man from the *'Daily Sketch'* had been the previous evening, his response was, "Done again!" It would appear that even in 1917 there was rivalry amongst the press. The reporter became quite cross and was even more annoyed when Jane Bonner refused to have her photograph taken, her patience no doubt wearing thin. The reporter went outside to photograph the farm and when Aunt Helen found him at the back of the house, she asked him if he would be so kind as to take photographs of the front of the house rather than milk churns and farm buildings!

Both local and national press reported the news of the award of Gus' VC but the front page headlines and full story would have to wait until the war had ended. For the time being the newspapers chose to elaborate on the very brief details given to them by the Admiralty, by making much of the fact that Gus was what they described as 'a mystery VC'; adding to the 'mystery' by highlighting the fact that he had both received his VC before it was announced in the *'London Gazette'* and been presented with it on a Sunday at Sandringham. Although it was widely reported at the time and since that Gus had received his VC on a Sunday, both the official documents and Gus' own account make it clear that he received the medal in the King's study at York Cottage Sandringham, shortly after 18.00 on Saturday October 6th 1917. The Court Circular dated 8th October 1917 reads:

> "York Cottage. Sandringham. Lieutenant Charles George Bonner RNR
> had the honour of being received by the King when His Majesty
> conferred on him the Victoria Cross in recognition of his conspicuous
> gallantry and consummate coolness and skill in action with an enemy
> submarine."

A typical example of how the press explained the lack of information was published in a local newspaper:

> "The exact details of the gallantry which earned the small bronze cross
> are shrouded in mystery so far as the general public is concerned.
> Were it advisable in the country's interests to allow publication of
> what happened on the waters of our restless frontier a short time ago,
> we feel sure that the pride of all citizens of the town and district
> would be increased by the thought of the superb coolness and

outstanding courage of one of our local men. But perhaps it were
better not so. Some day, when the enemy is beaten, the story may be
told. Suffice it for us to remember that the King has decorated our
local hero - not publicly with hundreds of others, but alone and on a
Sunday in the country, which, we believe, is an honour never before
conferred on a man."

Although this newspaper article contains the commonly held misconception that Gus received his VC on a Sunday, it does make a valid observation regarding the manner of the investiture. The majority of VC investitures take place at Buckingham Palace with the Sovereign having time for just a few words with each man and, although there may be instances of other investitures similar to the one which Gus Bonner was privileged to be granted, they are very unusual. He had the benefit of staying at Sandringham as the guest of the King and Queen, having a private investiture and chat with the King in his study, sitting next to HM at dinner, meeting various members of the Royal family and walking to church with them the following day. There cannot be many people who have been afforded such a privilege.

A further piece of information which would no doubt have been of interest to the press, is recorded in one of Sam Bonner's letters. He writes that Gus was expected at the Admiralty on the Monday morning after his investiture, following which he had lunch at the Carlton with Sir Ernest Shackleton whom he describes as, 'the great explorer.' Whether Gus knew Ernest Shackleton, a fellow master mariner, or they had just run into one another at the Admiralty, is not explained.

CONGRATULATIONS.

Gus kept many of the letters of congratulation which arrived at Manor Farm, including one from Walsall Council informing him that they had passed a formal resolution thanking him on behalf of the citizens of Walsall for his distinguished gallantry. The *'Walsall Pioneer'* newspaper wrote that the resolution was 'carried with acclamation,' and went on to say:

"Our human nature might at times be very weak and irresolute
but, when we read of such deeds we realise how, when it arrived
at its supreme test, human nature was capable of rising to the
utmost supreme heights of courage and resolution, and we
realised too, how in the face of danger men could make and carry
out decisions upon which the gravest issues of life depended."

Furness Withy, the company whom Gus worked for immediately prior to the outbreak of war, sent a congratulatory letter with more than twenty signatories, part of which read:

"This war has produced many heroes, but out of the numberless
hosts now engaged therein, the holders of the time-honoured
token are still few, and although details of the event have not yet
been made public, we have no doubt they would cause the hearts
of us all to swell with pride that one of the boys of the old 'Johnson
Line' should have so fully upheld the dignity and traditional bravery
of his race at such a time of crisis."

The secretary of the *Conway* also wrote of the ship's pride in one of her former cadets, whilst another letter, from the headmaster of Bishop Vesey's School, is of particular interest; not so much because of its content but because of the sender. The headmaster wrote:

The Imperial Merchant Service Guild

(BRITISH CERTIFICATED CAPTAINS AND OFFICERS.)

TELEPHONE NOS.:
8971 & 8972 BANK, LIVERPOOL.
3881 AVENUE, LONDON
1813 CARDIFF.
36 SOUTH SHIELDS.
52 CORPORATION, HULL.
4291 CENTRAL, GLASGOW.
Chief Assistant Secretary : (TEMPORARILY VACANT.)

Solicitors at
Most Leading
Seaports at
Home and
Abroad.

MSG

Over 400 Agents
Ashore and Afloat.
Agents at
Seaports throughout
the World.

ADDRESS TELEGRAMS:
DOLPHIN, LIVERPOOL.
GUILDCRAFT, LONDON.
DOLPHIN, CARDIFF.
DOLPHIN, SOUTHSHIELDS.
GUILDCRAFT, HULL.
DOLPHIN, GLASGOW.

Secretary: Mr. T. W. MOORE, F.R.G.S.,
Lieutenant, Royal Naval Reserve (Honorary).
Assistant Secretary : Lieut. G. B. SAY, R.N.V.R.
Cashier: Mr. C. K. MITCHELL.

HEAD OFFICES:
THE ARCADE, LORD STREET, LIVERPOOL.
OTHER OFFICES :
Dixon House, Lloyd's Avenue, London, E.C.
Colum Buildings, Mount Stuart Square, Cardiff.
Old Town Hall, South Shields.
41, King Edward Street, Hull.
Baltic Chambers, 50, Wellington Street, Glasgow.

M.K.

8th October, 1917.

To avoid unnecessary search and delay in reply, it is particularly requested that Members
when writing will give their Rotation Numbers.

Dear Lieutenant Bonner,

It is with feelings of sincere gratification
that we learn to-day of the coveted honour of the Victoria Cross
being conferred upon you by His Majesty.   This incident will
add still greater lustre to the already proud records of the
profession which we represent, and on behalf of the Imperial
Merchant Service Guild I beg to convey to you our very hearty
congratulations.

Yours faithfully,

J. W. Moore M.B.E.

Hon.Lieut.R.N.R.
Secretary.

Lieut. C. G. Bonner, V.C., D.S.C., R.N.R.,

*One of the many letters of congratulation Gus received
following the award of his Victoria Cross.*

"May I be allowed as Headmaster of one of your old schools to
congratulate you very heartily on the high honours you have gained
for conspicuous gallantry in the service of your country....
You may not realise what a thrill of pride has gone through the
school to know that one of the 'old boys' has gained the most
coveted distinction."

Both the writer of the letter, Herbert Jerrard, and Bishop Vesey's School, were to experience a further, 'thrill of pride,' when his own son Lieut. Alan Jerrard RFC, another former pupil, was awarded the VC less than six months later. Twenty year old Lieut. Jerrard received the award following his involvement in a combat mission over Italy which eventually ended with him being shot down and taken prisoner. In 1920, at the unveiling of the school's war memorial, plaques were dedicated to both VCs. One read:

> "This tablet is erected by the Governors to commemorate the award
> of the Victoria Cross to Lieutenant Charles George Bonner DSC RNR.
> for conspicuous bravery in the action between 'HMS Dunraven' and
> a German submarine on 8th of August 1917."

Gus would later serve as Vice-President of the school's old boys association.

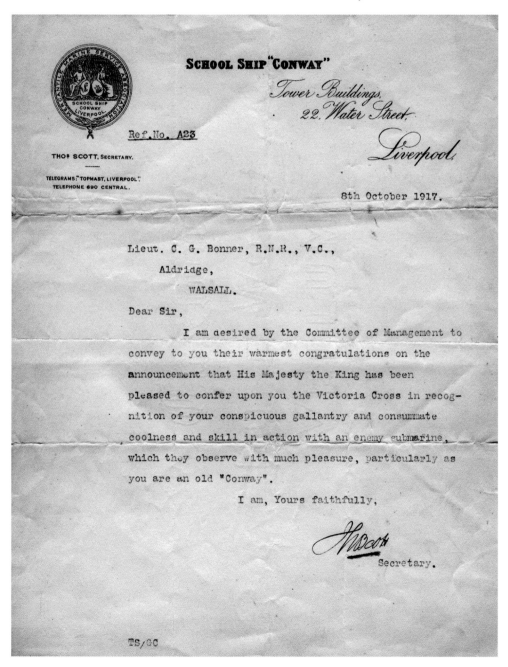

The Management Committee of the 'Conway'
passed on their warmest congratulations.

HOMECOMING.

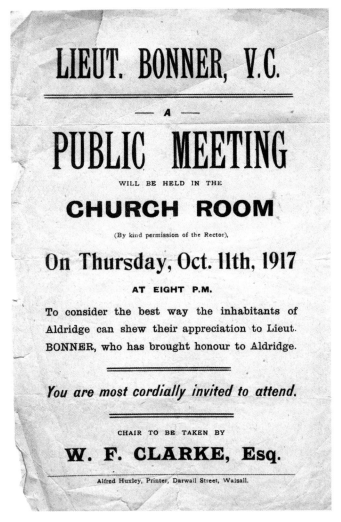

LIEUT. BONNER, V.C.

— A —

PUBLIC MEETING

WILL BE HELD IN THE

CHURCH ROOM

(By kind permission of the Rector).

On Thursday, Oct. 11th, 1917

AT EIGHT P.M.

To consider the best way the inhabitants of Aldridge can shew their appreciation to Lieut. BONNER, who has brought honour to Aldridge.

You are most cordially invited to attend.

CHAIR TO BE TAKEN BY

W. F. CLARKE, Esq.

Alfred Huxley, Printer, Darwall Street, Walsall.

Just five days after Gus received his VC, this hastily arranged meeting resulted in a testimonial fund numbering more than 350 subscribers.

On Thursday October 11th a public meeting was held at the church rooms in Aldridge in order to consider how the inhabitants of the village could best show their appreciation to the local hero. A testimonial fund was set up, with the list of subscribers reaching more than three hundred and fifty, including many well-known local names and relatives of men who had already made the supreme sacrifice.

Aunt Helen's diary records that three ladies went off to Birmingham on Friday morning to choose a silver tea and coffee service which was to be presented to Gus on his return. It would appear that one of these ladies was not very popular with the other two, but they seemed to have called a temporary truce in order to carry out the important task which they had been given; Aunt Helen remarking that they came back practically with their arms around each other. However hostilities were resumed a few days later when one of the ladies, who apparently knew Gus only slightly, began telling everyone in the village that she used to tuck him in bed when he was a child and that he was a chubby little thing. This provoked great indignation, with two other ladies claiming that it was they who put little Gus to bed!

Over the next few days the family became increasingly anxious about when, or indeed whether, Gus would be coming home. The people of Aldridge were constantly asking when they would see the local hero. Aunt Helen wrote:

> "Aldridge and Walsall had made up their minds that he must arrive at Walsall at 3pm, be escorted to Aldridge, taken to the church rooms or outside for the presentation. Village to be decorated etc etc."

During the weekend of the13th and 14th she wrote:

> "Rumours that Gus was at Minstead and dining with the Smiths (on) Sunday, so arrangements were made to have the presentation on Sunday.
> Sunday 14th. No letter from Gus nor Cissie. People pouring in to ask if we had heard. Arrangements made to meet the 10 o'clock train. All the Manor House and Miss Cooke's soldiers to form a guard of honour. People swarming on the Station bridge and people

THE MAYOR'S PARLOUR,
COUNCIL HOUSE,
WALSALL.

T/BMD

23rd.October,1917.

Lieutenant C.G.Bonner,V.C.,
ALDRIDGE.

Dear Sir,

     I have pleasure in bringing to your notice
the following copy resolution which was unanimously
passed at a meeting of the Walsall Town Council held
yesterday :-

    "That this Council,on behalf of the inhabit-
"ants of Walsall generally,places on record
"its deep appreciation of the distinguished
"gallantry which led to the award of the
"Victoria Cross by His Majesty the King to
"Lieutenant Bonner of Aldridge; it very
"warmly congratulates both Lieutenant Bonner
"and Aldridge on the winning by him of this
"signal honour and offers him their very best
"wishes for his future career."

    I sincerely hope that your father is making
a good recovery.

    Tendering you my own personal congratulations
and best wishes,

               I am,
             Yours faithfully,

                  Mayor.

*Walsall Council passed a resolution expressing
their deep appreciation of Gus' gallantry.*

> pouring up to the church room. Pa inclined to swear, Ma inclined
> to tears! Mrs Aston rushed to say Gus was not in Walsall. Mrs ??
> stamped her foot and all were disappointed."

One of the last entries in her diary for that weekend records:

> "A lovely day it was for the VC who never came!"

On Monday morning Jane and Helen busied themselves making a laurel wreath to decorate the front door
of Manor Farm ready for the home-coming, also finding time to see the silver tea and coffee service which
was being displayed in a glass case in a local shop window. Then, at last, Gus' long awaited letter arrived.
Having read it, Aunt Helen wrote:

"We are now looking and longing for the VC."

The local press reported that the people of Aldridge were, 'waiting with unconcealed excitement and impatience to lionise their hero.' He was expected on Saturday 20th October, so once again plans were made for the Local Volunteers to line the streets and provide a guard of honour from the railway station to Manor Farm. The *'Walsall Observer'* reported that Gus managed to escape a public demonstration by arriving four days earlier than expected and two hours before his last minute telegram said he would. Far from being critical, the journalist saw this as a further opportunity for praise saying:

" In Lieutenant Bonner, as in most heroes, the quality of courage is
ennobled by the twin virtue of modesty."

A public meeting was hastily arranged for the following day and although Samuel Bonner was ill and unable to attend the village's tribute to his son, Gus was accompanied by his wife, mother and sister to a crowded and enthusiastic meeting. When they arrived at the hall, which was decorated with a profusion of flags and bunting, he received a standing ovation followed by a chorus of, 'For He's a Jolly Good Fellow.' After the singing of the National Anthem apologies were given for Mr Marriott, Dr Jones and the Mayor of Walsall, Councillor S.M. Slater who had sent a telegram which read:

"Extremely regret I cannot attend tonight's gathering. I join in
recognition of the splendid courage which won Lieut. Bonner the
Victoria Cross. I congratulate him very warmly and Walsall
congratulates its near neighbour."

Local newspapers report Gus looking bronzed and well, although somewhat ill at ease, as speaker after speaker sang his praises; one saying that he recalled him coming to Aldridge as a babe in arms and that he was pleased to see how he had thrived in the village in a manner which was a credit to his country, adding that it was gratifying to know that Aldridge produced such men.

Reverend Tarleton, vicar of the Parish Church, said that Aldridge, "had leapt into world-wide fame" because of Gus and that he had given the young people of the Empire an example which would inspire them. The enthusiastic audience, which included a number of wounded servicemen, greeted every compliment with either applause, shouts of 'hear, hear' or loud cheering, and it was quite clear from the newspaper reports of the event that Gus was amazed at the reception he had received.

Although the awarding of a VC was not a common event, Gus had served with four others who had won the nations highest award for valour and did not, therefore, have any particular celebrity status in Plymouth or Queenstown. But for the people of a small village such as Aldridge with a population of around 3,000, Gus Bonner was a celebrity and the award of his VC gave the villagers something to celebrate. Like so many villages, towns and cities throughout the world, Aldridge had suffered greatly during the war. By the time of this hastily convened meeting in October 1917, forty men of the village had already lost their lives; by the end of the war the total had reached sixty. In the midst of so much sadness, Bonner's VC was something for the people of Aldridge to celebrate, and celebrate they did!

He was presented with the silver tea and coffee service by Reverend Tarleton who said that being asked to make such a presentation was one of the greatest honours he had ever had, adding:

"It is not the least in our minds to put a price on what you have done.
This is simply a small token of what we feel towards you, everyone of us,
from the bottom of our hearts, and something which will remind you of the

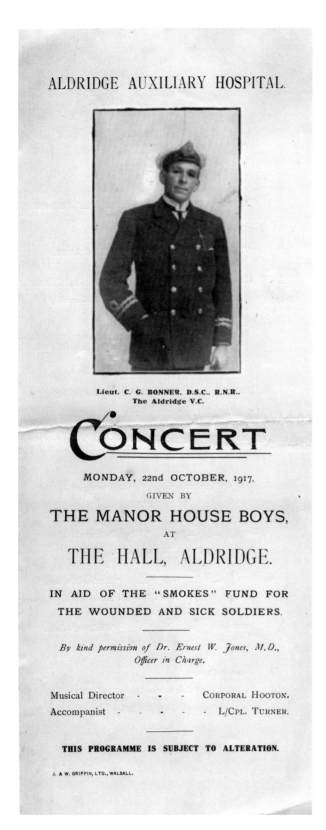

ALDRIDGE AUXILIARY HOSPITAL.

Lieut. C. G. BONNER, D.S.C., R.N.R.,
The Aldridge V.C.

CONCERT

MONDAY, 22nd OCTOBER, 1917,

GIVEN BY

THE MANOR HOUSE BOYS,

AT

THE HALL, ALDRIDGE.

IN AID OF THE "SMOKES" FUND FOR
THE WOUNDED AND SICK SOLDIERS.

*By kind permission of Dr. Ernest W. Jones, M.D.,
Officer in Charge.*

Musical Director - - - CORPORAL HOOTON.
Accompanist - - - - L/CPL. TURNER.

THIS PROGRAMME IS SUBJECT TO ALTERATION.

J. & W. GRIFFIN, LTD., WALSALL.

*A photograph of Gus was used to promote
a concert in aid of the Aldridge Auxiliary Hospital,
of which his mother was a keen supporter.*

feeling of love and admiration which you have created in everyone in Aldridge, and which will last as long as you live, because of what you have done for us and the world."

The salver of the tea and coffee service was engraved as follows:

"Presented to Lieutenant Charles George Bonner VC, by friends in Aldridge and others as a token of their admiration of his conspicuous gallantry, their pleasure that The Sovereign has recognised it, and their hope that he may have a long and happy life in the service of the country he has served so well."

The audience gave a standing ovation and as Gus stood up to reply the *'Walsall Observer'* reported:

"The man who faced deadly peril on the water with an iron nerve, quailed before the storm of cheers he had to face from a public platform."

Gus warned his audience that they would be disappointed by his reply adding:

"I can't attempt to thank you enough for your reception or your elaborate present. It has quite staggered me altogether. I was not expecting any such thing."

He then went on to pay tribute to the people of Aldridge; with the evening ending with three cheers for each of the family in turn and several choruses of 'For He's a Jolly Good Fellow.'

All too soon the brief visit to Aldridge came to an end. To say that Gus had had an eventful few months was something of an understatement and, as he prepared to go back to sea as captain of the *Eilian*, a further piece of news must have caused all manner of emotions: Cissy was pregnant.

Telegraphic & Cable Address:-
"HENCHMAN, LIVERPOOL."

Telephone Nº 8948 Bank.

Johnston Line Limited,

Managers:- FURNESS WITHY & Cº LIMITED.

American, Mediterranean, Black Sea and Danube Lines of Steamers,

Regular Line of Steamers
FROM
ANTWERP, SWANSEA AND LIVERPOOL
TO
PIRÆUS, VOLO, SALONICA, BOURGAS, VARNA,
CONSTANTZA, SULINA, GALATZ AND BRAILA.
LIVERPOOL TO BALTIMORE.
LONDON TO BOSTON.

REFERENCE

Your ....

Our ....

Royal Liver Building,

Liverpool, October 19th 1917.

Dear Mr. Bonner,

It is with feelings of the greatest
pride that we hasten to offer you our heartiest
congratulations on your having secured the highest
honour that could fall to the lot of man, viz:-
the "Victoria Cross."

This War has produced its many heroes,
but out of the numberless hosts now engaged therein, the
holders of the time-honoured token are still few, and
although details of the event have not yet been made
public, we have no doubt they would cause the hearts of
us all to swell with pride that one of the boys of the
old "Johnston Line" should have so fully upheld the
dignity and traditional bravery of his race at such a
time of crisis.

It is exceedingly difficult to express in
words what we all feel at this juncture, but we are proud
that during all our business careers we have been
associated with one who so unselfishly placed his
country first and whose efforts have been such as to
have justly merited so great an honour at the hands of
our esteemed and respected King.

Congratulatory letters such as this one, which had more that 20 signatories, continued to arrive at Manor Farm for several weeks following the award of Gus' VC.

Chapter 7

EILIAN: GUS IN COMMAND

Four days after his very warm and lively reception in Aldridge, Gus was back in Devonport - making his will! The document was signed on the 21st October 1917 and witnessed by Lieutenant Frame DSC RNR, who had served with Gus on *Dunraven*, and by Second Lieutenant Ernest Hutchison who gave his home address as Williamstown, Australia. Cissy was the sole beneficiary and executrix. Gus had had a very narrow escape on *Dunraven* and, with two other Q-ship captains having lost their lives in just one week, it was vital that he should provide for his wife and unborn child in the event of his death.

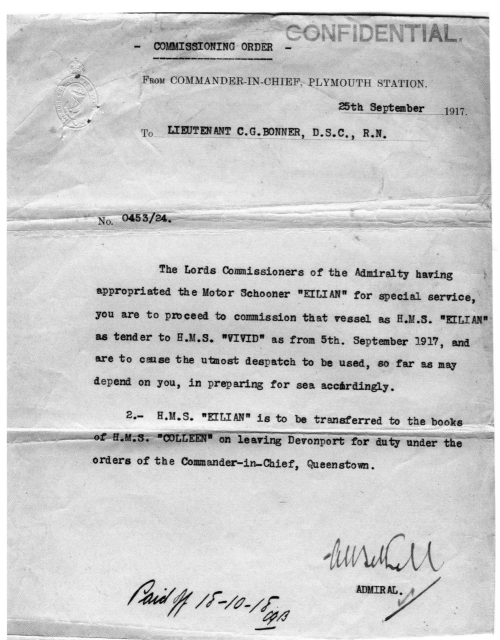

Gus' commissioning order for the Q-ship 'Eilian.'

Acting on the recommendation of Gordon Campbell, the Admiralty appointed Gus to HMS *Eilian*, a three-pole masted schooner of a hundred and forty tons built of steel by William Thomas of Amlwch, Anglesey in 1908. Her dimensions were 102.6ft x 21.9ft x 9.4ft. Pre-war records show her carrying various cargoes such as oats, coal, gravel and clay, up and down the coast but on the 8th September 1917 her owner, Hugh Hughes, was required to deliver her to Devonport for her re-fit as a Q-ship. Naval records show that she was fitted with sliding wooden screens which concealed two 12-pounder guns and a Lewis Gun. Her bow was strengthened to enable her to ram a U-boat, should the opportunity present itself. According to Jane Bonner's letters, all of the *Eilian's* crew had served with Gus on the *Dunraven*; William Williams, the *Pargust* VC, was one of them.

THE TIDE BEGINS TO TURN.

Although it is an over-simplification to say that it was the convoy system alone which finally gave the Allies the upper hand in the battle against the U-boat, it did play a significant part. There is a great deal of evidence to suggest that German submariners disliked having to attack a convoy; the main reasons being that destroyer escorts were always ready to ram a U-boat or pepper the sea with depth charges. Depth charges did not need to score a direct hit to cause major problems for a submarine and the effect on the morale and mental state of the men who had to withstand such an attack is well documented. The arrival of American destroyers meant that the pressure on the British Navy to provide escorts had eased and, by September, losses of merchant ships had been reduced to half what they had been in April.

The 'Eilian.'
(Courtesy of 'An Account Of The Motor-Vessel Eilian' by Peter R. Newcombe.)

Another benefit of the convoy system is that instead of having an ocean full of individual ships, with the odds of spotting a likely target quite high, the convoy system meant that U-boats could roam for days in a seemingly empty ocean, whilst large convoys often reached their destination without coming within the sight of a submarine. One author likened the battle between U-boat and merchant vessels as being akin to wolves attacking sheep, suggesting that wolves could roam as much as they liked: if they were prevented from reaching the sheep their presence meant little. U-boats did attack convoys but met with only limited success and so they turned some of their attention to 'picking off' smaller vessels in coastal waters. Smaller vessels such as the *Eilian*.

Another view of the 'Eilian'. The photograph is believed to have been taken in Penzance.

In 1919 a Committee of Enquiry in Berlin asked senior naval personnel to account for the failure of their U-boat campaign in 1917. Their response was that they had underestimated the number of U-boats and crew they would lose through the various anti-submarine methods employed by the Allies. Germany had calculated that they would lose up to three submarines a month but by the Spring of 1918 they were losing that many in a week. At the enquiry Admiral von Capelle was asked why there had not been sufficient U-boats in service when the campaign of unrestricted warfare began in February 1917. He said that the dockyards had been stretched to capacity by the need to repair the German High Seas Fleet following the Battle of Jutland, a battle hailed by Germany as a victory but possibly, it might be suggested, at the expense of the success of the U-boat war.

Gordon Campbell was of the opinion that the introduction of the convoy system meant that the Q-ship had had its day. Gus was to captain the *Eilian* for a further year under difficult and dangerous conditions and, although the introduction of the convoy system had begun to turn the tide in favour of the Allies by the time he took up his command, U-boats were still both active and successful. In December 1917, Germany's U-boats destroyed almost 400,000 tons of shipping: less than their target of 600,000 but still a significant amount. Added to this was the increasing threat of an Irish rebellion which resulted in the soldiers who were based at Queenstown being put on a state of high alert in case of an attempt to disrupt naval operations. Queenstown was, as ever, a dangerous place to be and, with the prospect of another harsh winter ahead, Admiral Bayly sent a memorandum to all of his ships in which he said:

"The winter is now approaching, and with storms and thick weather
the enemy shows an intention to strike harder and more often; but
I feel perfect confidence in those who are working with me that we
shall wear him down and utterly defeat him in the face of all difficulties."

MISSING MAIL.

For any serviceman, letters and parcels from home were of the utmost importance, but the rather unusual name of Gus' ship seemed to be causing his mail to go astray. On November 20th he wrote to his parents from the *Eilian*:

> "Been expecting a letter from Cis for some days, but up to now not
> turned up, neither has the parcel (wrist-watch) you wrote about. Am
> afraid the mail for my ship is going to a ship called *Eileen* whose
> whereabouts I do not know, so please be careful to write the ship's name
> very distinctly or goodness knows where the letters will go."

The wrist-watch which Gus refers to in his letter was bought with some of the money which had been collected in Aldridge following the award of his VC; the outstanding balance of the collection being used to purchase £40 of War Loans in Cissy's name. As an officer of His Majesty's Navy, Gus was not allowed to accept the money himself. The saga of the missing wrist-watch continued in his letter dated 25th December 1917. He wrote:

> "Dear Father and Mother. In port for an hour or two, so just a few lines
> hoping that you've been able to get some sort of decent Xmas day in
> spite of the war. Do hope that Pa is looking after himself in spite of
> the cold weather we're having now, hope it won't be a very bad winter
> after all. The war still appears to be dragging along in spite of all our
> victories but I think we're well through the worst of it now. Last time
> I saw Capt. C. he had just been to Buckingham Palace and he told me
> that the King asked him how I was getting on etc. I did not expect six
> months ago to have H.M. asking about me!! The watch still hasn't
> turned up so far, hope that it hasn't been pinched or I suppose there'll
> be a ... (sic) of a row somewhere. Good-bye and God bless you both.
> Will write at the next opportunity.
> I remain, ever your most loving son.
> Gus."

Unfortunately the tale of the missing wrist-watch cannot be brought to a conclusion as it is not mentioned again in any correspondence.

Christmas 1917 appears to have been a difficult one for Jane Bonner. Early in December Cis had written to her expressing concern that Gus was looking very tired and that he was finding that 'the constant watching,' as captain of his own Q-ship, was, 'getting on his nerves.' Then followed three weeks when no one in the family heard from Gus, always hoping for the best but secretly fearing the worst. There were all too many incidences of Q-ships and their crew putting to sea and then simply never being heard of again. His letter came as a great relief at a Christmas which Jane describes as the quietest they had ever had. She must have been all too aware of the empty chairs around the Christmas table and this politically astute woman also knew that the war was far from won. She ended her Christmas letter to her daughters in unusually subdued fashion by saying:

> "Well, I must say goodbye now. I hope that we shall soon get better
> news from all parts."

AMERICA'S Q-SHIP.

While Gus was using his few hours in port on Christmas Day to write to his parents, up at Admiralty House Lewis Bayly was playing host to American Rear-Admiral William Sims. Two days after Christmas they were to witness the launch of the USA's first Q-ship. William Sims was of the opinion that Q-ships played an important role in the battle against Germany's U-boats. Writing after the war he said:

> "It is desirable to repeat and emphasise that the most important
> accomplishment of the mystery ships was really not the actual
> sinking of submarines, but their profound influence upon the tactics
> of the U-boats."

Regarding America's desire for her own Q-ship he wrote:

> "So great was the desire of our people to take some part in the mystery
> ship campaign that I took steps to satisfy their legitimate ambition."

The original intention was for the British Navy to give the *Pargust* to America but as she was still undergoing repairs another vessel, the *Arvonian*, was chosen. She was given the name USS *Santee* and, with Gordon Campbell advising on her re-fit, she became the 'last word' in Q-ships. It would have been a strange coincidence had the *Pargust* been the chosen vessel as the captain of America's first Q-ship was to be Commander David Hanrahan. It was his ship, the USS *Cushing*, which had provided the escort for the *Pargust* following her encounter with UC 29 in which Gus won his DSC. Such was the interest in the *Santee* that Rear-Admiral Sims recorded:

> "Practically all the officers and men of the forces based at Queenstown
> clamoured for this highly interesting though hazardous service."

One evening at the end of December the *Santee* sailed from Queenstown bound for Bantry Bay to carry out extensive training. She had only been out of port for five hours when she was torpedoed and, although inexperienced, the crew carried out the 'abandon ship' procedure perfectly, with those left on board staying hidden, waiting for the U-boat's next move. They kept a very careful watch for five hours before accepting that their enemy was long gone and then *Santee* was towed back to port.

PRIDE IN HIS WORK.

On one occasion whilst they were in harbour at Kingstown (now called Dun Laoghaire), customs officials informed Gus that they intended to search the *Eilian*. To refuse would have invited unwanted attention and so Gus and his men waited with bated breath whilst their ship was searched. It is a credit to the men who fitted the Q-ships that the customs men did not find the concealed guns, passing the *Eilian* as 'safe.' Of course it could be suggested that perhaps the officials were not doing their job as well as they ought but even Rear-Admiral William Sims had difficulty in seeing through the disguise of a Q-ship. On one occasion he viewed the vessels at Queenstown through his binoculars and not only failed to spot the hidden guns but even when he was invited on board he was still unable to find their location. He wrote:

> "We searched carefully but we were utterly unable to discover
> where the guns were."

Admiral Bayly described another occasion when William Sims visited HMS *Dunraven*:

"Sims was leaning against a bulkhead when it gave way and disclosed a gun, and later he was holding onto a rail to look at something when it came away in his hand. I think after a short time he was quite glad to leave the ship."

This photograph of Gus was probably taken in the garden of Manor Farm.
It is dated October 20th 1917.

Such was Gus' confidence in the innocent appearance of his own Q-ship that on one occasion he challenged a fellow naval officer to spot the *Eilian* from six vessels which were in port. After careful examination and four guesses the officer finally selected the right ship!

Now that Gus had command of his own ship he came into much more regular contact with Lewis Bayly, by now sixty years old and promoted to Admiral; it was a friendship which would last for many years. Lewis Bayly made it known that he was available to his officers at any time of the day or night if he was needed, even turning over part of the grounds of Admiralty House to them so that they could have somewhere for a little peace and privacy. His letters to Gus show him to be a man of modesty, integrity, loyalty and pragmatism. Admiral Sir Roger Backhouse said of him:

> "To those officers and men who served under him he was as loyal a friend as could be found, provided only that they had his confidence and that he believed that they were imbued with the same purpose as himself. He could not tolerate slackness or inefficiency, and he was not prepared to put up with second best."

Gus was clearly impressed by Admiral Bayly on one of the first occasions they dined together in November 1917. He wrote to his parents:

> "The Admiral here (Bayly) has been awfully nice, had me to dinner and been as good as gold all through. He will be the man to take Jellicoe's place bye and bye, so is some man and very, very clever."

Admiral Bayly's niece, Violet Voysey, was also very kind to Gus: offering to make and repair clothes for both him and his men.

During his early months as a Q-ship captain, Gus was hopeful of encountering a submarine. In a letter to his parents he wrote:

> "I am sorry to say that I missed getting a sub by about 15 minutes on my way here (no fault of mine), but we are going out tomorrow and hope to make up for it, perhaps get two."

Over the coming months Gus grew increasingly frustrated with the lack of action and wrote to his former captain for advice. Gordon Campbell knew only too well how he was feeling. He wrote to tell Gus that in his early days as a Q-ship commander, he had been U-boat hunting for nine months without even seeing a submarine, fearing that the war would end before he had the opportunity to fire a shot. He assured Gus that he was doing everything he could and that the lack of 'action' did not reflect badly on him, his crew or his ship. Rear-Admiral Sims likened a Q-ship to a patient fisherman saying:

> "Perhaps the most distressing part of existence on one of these ships was its monotony. Day would follow day, week would follow week and sometimes months would pass without their encountering a single submarine. The mystery boat was a patient fisherman, constantly expecting a bite, and frequently going for long periods without even the slightest nibble."

The fact was that the introduction of the convoy system meant that the situation had changed and the experience of the *Eilian* was one which was shared by other Q-ships during what was to be the final year of the war. The website naval-history.net records that not a single U-boat was confirmed as being sunk by a Q-ship in 1918 although there were two unconfirmed sinkings; this contrasts with six confirmed and two unconfirmed German losses in 1917.

Gus wrote, "Gun's crew HMS 'Eilian' August 1918" on the reverse of this photograph.
Three further images from the ship can be seen in Chapter 3.

Whilst much has been written about the dramatic encounters involving Q-ships, it is usually only the eye-witness accounts which recall the other aspects of their work: the days, weeks, months and sometimes years spent at sea in a permanent state of readiness. Their enemy was a formidable one and for the men of the decoy ships their only chance of survival as bait for a U-boat was to stay ever vigilant: always behaving as though they were being watched. To let their guard slip could all too easily result in their deaths. The strain meant that some men had to be moved to other work, whilst many of those who served on Q-ships for long periods of time would feel the effects for the rest of their lives Correspondence between Gus and Lewis Bayly after the war had ended shows that even Gordon Campbell, whom Admiral Sims described as:

> "absolutely lacking in any sign of nerves and seemingly created for
> Q-ship work,"

had suffered ill health as a result of his Q-ship experiences. Another man who was to suffer from the strain of the work was Seaman William Williams VC who served with Gus on *Pargust*, *Dunraven* and finally *Eilian*, having served on His Majesty's Q-ships for a total of three years. He was the most highly decorated seaman of the Great War: being awarded the DSM in the action against UC 83 which had won Campbell his VC, the Victoria Cross and Medalle Militaire on the *Pargust*, and a bar to his DSM for manning the defensive gun on *Dunraven* whilst fully exposed to enemy fire. And yet it would appear that the strain of Q-ship work took its toll on even this strong, fit and very brave young man. He was discharged as, 'medically unfit for further service,' just one month after his 28th birthday and five days before the Armistice was signed.

A senior member of the staff of Admiralty House, Paymaster-Commander H.R. Russell, saw first hand the strain which Q-ship worked entailed. He wrote to Gus after the war:

> "Those of us who had to occupy office chairs during the war could not
> perhaps fully realise what you fellows afloat had to put up with in the
> way of discomforts and long spells at sea varied only by the lurid
> intervals when you met a submarine. Now that the stories of some of the
> submarine engagements have been published everyone will realise how
> fully you earned your honours in action, but they will never know the
> long days spent watching and waiting in all weathers. The 'Special
> Service' officers and men will always know that they did at least as
> much towards winning the war as any soldiers in the hottest shore
> fighting."

AND I NAME THIS CHILD….

A very welcome interlude during Gus' final year on His Majesty's Q-ships came via a telegram dated 15th June 1918. No doubt mindful of the earlier difficulties regarding the distribution of mail to other ships with similar sounding names, the sender had the name of the ship written in large capital letters. Despite the fact that the name of the ship was, once again, spelt incorrectly, this all important telegram did manage to reach its destination. It read:

> "Son born 4-o-clock Both doing well Dr Fox"

Gus sent his reply the same day:

> "Wire received Delighted Will come home during the week Love Gus"

On 19th June he came home to see his wife and son and registered his son's birth with the Walsall Registrars; choosing the name Charles Gordon Bonner. It was decided that Cis would write to Gordon Campbell inviting him to be godfather. A few weeks later Gus wrote to say that Campbell was delighted to have been asked to be godfather but was disappointed that the baby would not bear the name Dunraven

The proud parents: Gus and Cissy with their son Gordon Dunraven Bonner.

as he believed that the name would one day be famous. Gordon Campbell and his wife had just suffered the loss of a stillborn son who, according to the letters which were exchanged between Gus and his family, would have been given the name Dunraven had he lived. It is a measure of the friendship which existed between the two men, that Gus and Cissy decided that she should go back to the Registrars and change their son's name to Gordon Dunraven Bonner. In the midst of his own sadness at the death of his son, Gordon Campbell was pleased to know that the name Dunraven would live on, and Mrs. Campbell wrote to Cis offering her very best wishes and congratulations to the new parents.

On hearing the news of the birth of her grandson, Jane Bonner wrote to her daughters to tell them the news. Gordon had been born in the Partridge family home, Minstead, and Jane said:

> "As soon as he was born Dr. Fox bellowed over the banister, 'Mrs P.
> A son. A little VC."

When Jane saw Gordon Dunraven for the first time, she was clearly very taken with him. She wrote:

> "He is a little darling. Such a good boy. The first good Bonner baby
> has a dear little round pink and white face, black hair and eyes, and
> looks so intelligent. I nursed him for quite a long time and he lay
> quiet, smiling and looking me up and down all the time."

Gus and Cissy's only child was baptised at Great Barr Parish Church on July 12th 1918; the baptism ceremony being conducted by the Reverend W.T Corfield, the vicar who had married them just a year earlier. A telegram dated July 12th from his proud godfather read:

> "Sorry I am not at your christening Be a good boy and grow up a brave
> man like your father he is at sea now thinking of you Best wishes
> your affectionate godfather Gordon Campbell"

Jane said of her grandson's behaviour at the ceremony:

> "Gordon was so sweet. He's like a little cherub. Slept until the water
> was put on, then he opened his eyes and gave such a long yawn in the
> Vicar's face. He was amused, as we all were."

Jane was equally delighted with a letter which Gus had received. She said:

> "Gus had a letter from the Admiral's niece (Miss Voysey) who keeps
> house for him. She said how proud the son would be to have such a
> Pa, and how much Admiral Bayly thinks of Gus."

Gus' parents also enquired as to whether he was in need of any money now that he had the extra responsibility of a child to care for. As a Q-ship officer he was earning twice the usual pay for a man of his rank and replied:

> "I am quite okay for money (never had so much in my life). I give
> Cis £28 a month and then she is able to get £2 a month for Gordon
> from the Admiralty until the war's over or he's 16 if it lasts that long."

Gordon Dunraven Bonner did not prove to be much of a drain on Admiralty finances. Within six months

Germany's gamble, that its unrestricted U-boat war would force the Allies to surrender before American troops could be transported to France in significant numbers, had failed. But, like millions of young couples who lived through what was described as the 'war to end all wars,' Gus and Cissy could scarce have imagined that they would live to see their own son called to serve in a second world war.

UNWELCOME PUBLICITY.

Capt. Gordon Campbell, V.C., D.S.O.   Petty Officer Pitcher, V.C.   Lieut. Bonner, V.C., D.S.C.

Sir Eric Geddes has disclosed a little part of the share the mystery ships have played in fighting and sinking German submarines. When the full story is told, here are three of the men whose deeds will send a thrill through the world. The British sailor is equal to any emergency.

Gus and Gordon Campbell were angry about Sir Eric Geddes' comments and the headlines which followed. (Courtesy of Associated Newspapers.)

At the beginning of August 1918 many national newspapers carried details of a speech which had been given by First Lord of the Admiralty, Sir Eric Geddes, to a large audience at the Palace Theatre, London. The speech gave some information about an action involving a Q-ship, giving a description of their method of operation and the type of personnel onboard. It would appear from the information contained in some of the newspaper reports that Geddes felt that there was no longer any need for the secrecy which had surrounded the work of the Q-ships. From Jane Bonner's letters to her daughters it is quite clear that Gus disagreed! He was still a serving naval officer in a war-zone, who found his photograph on the front pages of the national newspapers identifying him as someone who 'lured U-boats to their doom.' Gus wrote to his parents to tell them that he felt that Geddes had made a mistake in revealing details about the Q-ships; suggesting that Gordon Campbell was also angry about the revelations.

GOODBYE TO QUEENSTOWN.

During the month of August, a problem with the *Eilian* brought Gus to Liverpool for three weeks and he took the opportunity to find lodgings for Cissy, Gordon and his mother-in law; Mrs Partridge acting as babysitter thus enabling the new parents to spend some time together. In his next letter dated 20th of September, Gus wrote to his parents to tell them that he had left Queenstown:

> "I left Queenstown three days ago in a hurry-up job for where I am now
> and shall soon be over on the English coast again. Had a good time at
> Queenstown. The Admiral and his niece were very kind and nice, and
> the old fellow came on-board and sat in the wardroom for a while the
> day we were sailing (a great honour). All the other ships were very
> jealous about it."

At the end of October Jane Bonner wrote:

"Gus is on leave for two weeks. He has paid off his ramshackle old boat and has had the offer of another, I believe, to carry supplies for the Navy and it will be armed for subs as well."

By Command of the Commissioners for Executing the Office of Lord High Admiral of the United Kingdom of Great Britain and Ireland, &c.

C.W.

To *Lieutenant Charles G. Bonner*, V.C., D.S.C., R.N.R.

The Lords Commissioners of the Admiralty hereby appoint you *Temporary Lieutenant R.N.R.*

of His Majesty's Ship *"Aviator" in Command*

and direct you to repair on board that Ship at

Your appointment is to take effect from the *3rd November 1918.*

You are to acknowledge the receipt of this Appointment forthwith, addressing your letter to

taking care to furnish your address.

By Command of their Lordships.

H.M.S. "Aviator"

O. Murray

Admiralty, S.W. 1.

Gus' final command of the Great War was as captain of the store carrier HMS 'Aviator.'

The vessel Jane Bonner spoke about was *Aviator*, a store carrier. Official records show that Gus took charge of it on November 3rd and was home on leave on the day that the guns finally fell silent on the Western Front. He left *Aviator* on November 30th, being transferred to Devonport prior to what the Navy referred to as 'disposal.'

Admiral Bayly sent the following memorandum to all of the senior officers under his command:

> "After commanding the Coast of Ireland Station for three years I am
> very proud to be able to thank the Sloops, Trawlers, Minesweepers
> Drifters and Motor Launches, as well as the officers and ratings
> employed on shore, for the ability and energy with which they have
> fought the Country's enemies and have so materially assisted the
> Country's necessities to be brought safely home from overseas. Very
> many acts of bravery have been performed, and I deeply regret to say
> that many valuable lives have been lost; but all hands have followed
> the great traditions of the sea in their contempt of danger, their
> readiness for responsibility, and their sympathetic help for the
> suffering."

THE EFFECTIVENESS OF Q-SHIPS.

Several writers who have considered the bare statistics of the Great War have drawn the conclusion that Q-ships were both ineffective and ill-conceived. However, several influential figures, including Gordon Campbell and William Sims have argued that the principal contribution made by the Q-ships was not the actual destruction of the enemy but the effect that their existence had on the behaviour of the U-boats. Rear-Admiral Sims said:

> "The mere fact that a number of Q-ships were at sea, even if they did
> not succeed in sinking many submarines, forced the Germans to make
> a radical change to their tactics."

He also cited the fact that German newspapers and magazines devoted a great deal of space to these so called 'barbaric trap-ships.' This, he said, was evidence that the enemy were very disturbed by their presence.

Consider for a moment the time taken and caution exercised by Reinhold Salzwedel in his encounter with the *Dunraven*. His own report shows that the actual encounter took around six hours, with a further three or four hours spent in observation of the attempts to save the ship. Had Q-ships not existed he would have had no reason to be so cautious, enabling him to sink the *Dunraven* and then hunt for other prey. The report which Gordon Campbell received from a German source concerning the encounter stated;

> "Although Salzwedel failed at first to detect the real nature of the steamer
> he acted from the start as carefully as if he had known she was a Q-ship."

Such a statement appears to reinforce both Sims and Campbell's' belief that the existence of Q-ships had an effect on the behaviour and tactics of every U-boat.

Gordon Campbell was critical of the Admiralty's use of Q-ships, believing that had they been used in large numbers at the start of the U-boat campaign, they would have been much more effective. As soon as the first unsuccessful action took place and a U-boat managed to return home with warnings about the British trap-ships, the chances of success were diminished. It could also be argued that little attention is paid to the number of U-boats which were damaged during the encounters and so had to return to their base for repairs rather than continue about their business of sinking merchant shipping. Gordon Campbell estimated that approximately sixty U-boats suffered damage due to the actions of a Q-ship. Campbell also believed that their existence had an effect on the morale of German seaman and it is easy to understand why. Q-ships came in many guises, from fishing smacks to colliers, so a U-boat crew would always have in their minds the possibility that the innocent-looking merchant ship which their captain had chosen to engage could well possess the capability of destroying them in minutes. This would put them under as much strain as that experienced by the men of the Q-ships, but there was one very important difference between them: the men of the Q-ships were all volunteers who not only chose that type of work but were chosen from a waiting list of others. U-boat men were not always volunteers.

The fact is no one can say with any degree of certainty whether the Q-ships were or were not an effective weapon against Germany's U-boats and the debate will no doubt continue. However, one thing that is beyond debate is the bravery of the men who served on them. Rear-Admiral Sims put it very well when he said:

> "We have laid great emphasis upon the brutalising aspects of the
> European War: it is well, therefore, that we do not forget that it had
> its more exalted phases. Human nature may at times have manifested
> itself in its most cowardly traits, though it also reached a level of
> courage which, I am confident, it has seldom attained in any other
> conflict, It was reserved for this desperate struggle to teach us how
> brave modern man could be."

PEACE AT LAST.

Those of us in the fortunate position not to have experienced war at first hand can only speculate as to how individuals felt on the day of the Armistice and during the days and months that followed. The men of the Q-ships had, of necessity, formed a bond which was difficult to break. Gordon Campbell had said that any one man could spoil the show and so each relied on the other for their survival, not just in the encounters with a U-boat but also in the long days and nights of watching and waiting. That reliance on a fellow human being was something which they were not likely to have experienced with such intensity before and probably wouldn't experience again.

Within a few days of the Armistice and as their stories were told to an eager press, Gus and his fellow VCs were to become national heroes. On the 16th November 1918 photographs of Gus and Gordon Campbell appeared on the front of the '*Daily Mirror*' under the headline 'Bravest of the Brave'. On another occasion photographs of all eight Q-ship VCs appeared in the same newspaper with a brief summary of each act of valour. The photograph of Gus was accompanied by a caption which read:

> Lieut. Charles George Bonner VC DSC RNR who was on the mystery ship
> *Dunraven* when, with blazing decks and exploding magazines, she continued
> her fight with the submarine until it was glad to escape.

It is doubtful whether anyone on *Dunraven* would have agreed with the final line of that caption: probably thinking that it was they who were glad to have escaped with their lives.

The Admiralty's official version of the actions for which the men of the Q-ships received the nation's highest honour was published in the 'London Gazette' a week after the Armistice. The national press seized on these basically factual reports and gave their own interpretation. One report, typical of many, read:

"In the whole splendid record of the British Navy there is no achievement more glorious than that of the Q-boats, of which something has just been disclosed in an Admiralty report. The story makes the best sea romances of fiction writers utterly tame by comparison. The heroism of the officers and men of these naval mystery ships in their fights with the Hun U-boats surpasses anything that could have been conceived to be within the compass of human self-sacrifice and endurance."

Gus did not want to return to the life of a merchant seaman and in a letter to Colonel Wigram, whom he had stayed with at Sandringham, he said that he was hoping to be given the command of an oiler (an auxiliary naval vessel for refuelling at sea). Colonel Wigram wrote in reply:

"My dear Bonner, I was pleased to hear from you and took the liberty of showing your letter to the King. We think that you deserve the very best you can get."

Gus' final conduct certificate, signed by Admiral Sir Lewis Bayly.

Gus knew that there was very little chance of the Navy finding a use for him now that the war was over as they were inundated with applications from other men making the same request, and so on 18th January 1919 Temporary Lieutenant Charles George Bonner was finally discharged from the Royal Naval Reserve. Lewis Bayly made a remark in his officer training book which read:

"Note. This officer has done exceptionally good service for which he
Has been awarded a V.C and D.S.C."

When war began Gus had been a single man training with the RNVR. By the end of it he was a husband and father who had met the King for himself, and whose story had appeared in the local, national and international press. He packed his things and left Devonport to begin a proper family life with his wife and son, no doubt thinking himself fortunate to have survived the most terrible war in history. Yet Gus Bonner's days of serving his country were not at an end; the skills and experience he was to gain during the inter-war years would prove to be of vital importance to the nation in the Second World War.

Chapter 8
A NEW CAREER

In March 1919, Gus returned to his pre-war post with the Liverpool based company Furness Withy, his first trip being on the SS *Wyncote* to the east coast of America however, in August of the same year, he embarked on a new career in marine salvage.

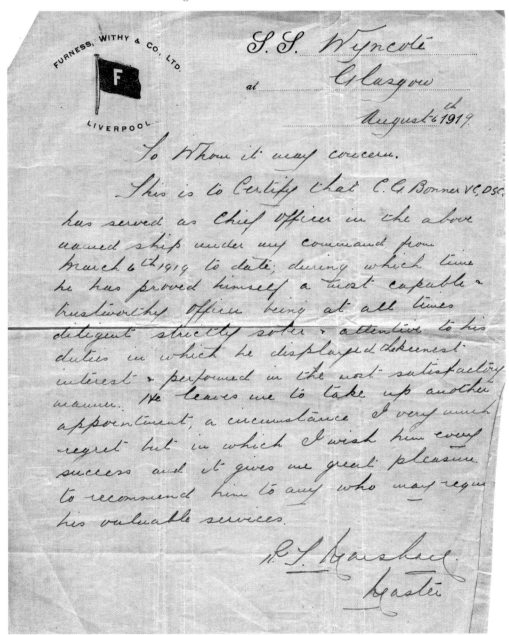

This was the final reference of Gus' career as a merchant seaman.

In the summer of 1919, Gus, Cissy and one year old Gordon moved to what was to be the family home for the rest of Gus' life: 12, Netherby Road, Edinburgh. He had been appointed to the position of assistant salvage officer with the Leith Salvage and Towage Company on a starting salary of £400 per annum.

By September this had risen to £450 and in January 1920 he was promoted to salvage officer with a salary of £500 plus 2½ % commission. Due to the somewhat unpredictable and sometimes dangerous nature of salvage work, he had to pay an additional premium of £5 per annum on his insurance policy with the Northern Assurance Company, in consideration of which he was allowed to follow the occupation of salvage officer and was permitted to dive but only occasionally.

After the Great War many new salvage companies had been formed and although some survived, a large number went into liquidation. Salvage work was not easy: each job was different and many factors could influence the outcome of the operation, such as the position, size, cargo and condition of the ship, as well as the weather and tide. A successful salvage officer needed to be a thorough seaman with a knowledge of scientific principles, engineering, naval architecture, maritime law and meteorology. He would also need to be able to command a group of men, have infinite patience and at the same time always have one eye on the cost of the operation. The owner of a ship may well want his vessel and cargo retrieved, but not if the cost of doing so was more than their value. The key to a good salvage operation was not just to recover the ship and its cargo but to do so in a cost-efficient manner. With many companies operating on what Gus referred to as a 'no cure, no pay' basis, it is small wonder that many of them failed. Something as simple as a change of tide or weather at a crucial moment could undo days of patient work, resulting in the loss of the ship and, therefore, no payment for the company. If a ship were to become a total loss under such circumstances, a salvage company also ran the risk of being sued for damages.! However, Gus was destined to carve out a very successful career in marine salvage and would once again find himself featured in newspapers and magazines.

Gus stayed in touch with many of the men from his Q-ship days, particularly Gordon Campbell - who was still a serving naval officer - and Lewis Bayly who had been retired. In a letter to Gus from his home in Devon, Admiral Bayly wrote:

> "I was sorry to leave the service, but having been told that there was
> no further intention of employing me, I saw no use in hanging on, so
> settled down in the country to try and expend my energies doing
> something useful."

GARDEN PARTY AT THE PALACE.

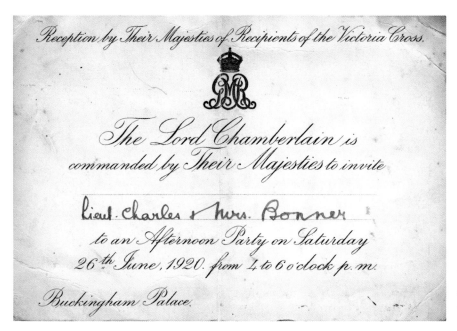

Gus and Cissy's
official invitation to
the afternoon party.

In June 1920 Gus and Cissy were given the opportunity of meeting up with several of Gus' old shipmates when they were invited to a garden party for the holders of the VC and their relatives which was to be held at Buckingham Palace. Gus and Cissy made the long journey down to London for what was described by one newspaper as, 'a gathering unique in our history.' At 12.30 on Saturday June 26th many of the three hundred or so VCs who had accepted the invitation and their guests gathered at Wellington Barracks, just

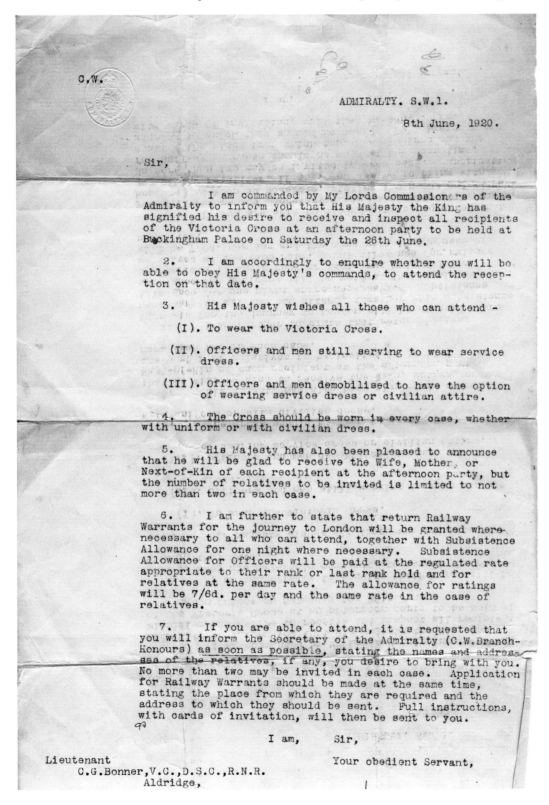

C.W.

ADMIRALTY. S.W.1.

8th June, 1920.

Sir,

I am commanded by My Lords Commissioners of the Admiralty to inform you that His Majesty the King has signified his desire to receive and inspect all recipients of the Victoria Cross at an afternoon party to be held at Buckingham Palace on Saturday the 26th June.

2. I am accordingly to enquire whether you will be able to obey His Majesty's commands, to attend the reception on that date.

3. His Majesty wishes all those who can attend -

(I). To wear the Victoria Cross.

(II). Officers and men still serving to wear service dress.

(III). Officers and men demobilised to have the option of wearing service dress or civilian attire.

4. The Cross should be worn in every case, whether with uniform or with civilian dress.

5. His Majesty has also been pleased to announce that he will be glad to receive the Wife, Mother, or Next-of-Kin of each recipient at the afternoon party, but the number of relatives to be invited is limited to not more than two in each case.

6. I am further to state that return Railway Warrants for the journey to London will be granted where necessary to all who can attend, together with Subsistence Allowance for one night where necessary. Subsistence Allowance for Officers will be paid at the regulated rate appropriate to their rank or last rank held and for relatives at the same rate. The allowance for ratings will be 7/6d. per day and the same rate in the case of relatives.

7. If you are able to attend, it is requested that you will inform the Secretary of the Admiralty (C.W.Branch-Honours) as soon as possible, stating the names and addresses of the relatives, if any, you desire to bring with you. No more than two may be invited in each case. Application for Railway Warrants should be made at the same time, stating the place from which they are required and the address to which they should be sent. Full instructions, with cards of invitation, will then be sent to you.

I am, Sir,

Lieutenant
  C.G.Bonner,V.C.,D.S.C.,R.N.R.
    Aldridge,

Your obedient Servant,

VCs received just two weeks notice of the intention to hold an afternoon party at Buckingham Palace.

two hundred yards away from the Palace, where they were given lunch and entertained by the Band of the Welsh Guards. Throughout the morning spectators had been arriving on the streets of London in order to pay their tribute to this assembly of heroes, thousands gathering outside the barracks and some even climbing the railings to get a better view. Although the event was strictly confined to VCs and their guests, the King was anxious that the public should have the opportunity of showing their appreciation and so a parade through the streets had been arranged for 15.00.

Gus chose to wear his uniform and, of course, his VC and DSC. The three other medals to which he was entitled - the 1914/15 Star, the British War Medal and the Victory Medal - had not yet been issued to him. Of the six surviving Q-ship VCs, only one, Ronald Stuart, was absent and after lunch while their guests made their way to the Palace, Gus, Gordon Campbell, William Williams, Ernest Pitcher and Harold Auten joined their fellow VCs for the parade. Not all of the VCs who accepted an invitation to the garden party were able to march. Eighty-seven year old Sir Dighton Probyn, whom Gus had met at Sandringham in 1917, had chosen, along with several others, to go straight to the Palace. Other elderly VCs and a number who were disabled were carried in a fleet of cars at the rear. As members of the 'Senior Service,' naval VCs were at the head of the parade and marched in rows of four, Gus being on the outside of the fourth row and so nearest the crowd.

The naval group preparing to march to Buckingham Palace. Gus is circled within the picture.
The bearded Ernest Pitcher is towards the rear of the parade. Gordon Campbell is two rows in front of him,
on the same row as Gus.
(Courtesy of Stephen Snelling.)

At 15.00, with the Band of the Welsh Guards at the front of the parade, Admiral of the Fleet, Sir Arthur Wilson VC, led a group of men from all walks of life through the streets of London. Some dressed in uniform and bedecked with medals, others in suits, straw boaters, trilbys or cloth caps, but all members of one of the most exclusive groups in the world: those whose bravery in the face of the enemy had earned them the Victoria Cross. As they emerged into Birdcage Walk, the huge crowd greeted them with a deafening roar, hats were tossed into the air and, as the column passed close enough for individuals to be recognised, the crowd called out the names of those whose faces had become familiar to them through the accounts of their deeds in national newspapers. Flowers were thrown, heads were bared and many in the crowd were crying. Perhaps they were overcome by the occasion or the sight of so many men wearing the nation's 'badge of courage'; or perhaps their thoughts were with those who had not returned from the world's most terrible war: those whose courage and service to their country had caused them to pay the ultimate price.

All manner of emotions were present on this June afternoon: euphoria, pride, sadness and gratitude to name but a few. At various places on the march the crowd were very vocal, whilst in other places an air of solemnity seemed to descend, with one VC remarking that it was not the loud cheers, clapping or throwing of flowers which moved himself and others to the brink of tears, but the spontaneous and silent baring of heads as a mark of respect.

Although the police had responsibility for security they did, on this occasion, allow some spectators to breach the cordon. One was a lady with a box of flowers which she was throwing towards the parade. The flowers were, however, falling short and so she was allowed through to deliver them to the VCs by hand. Another very popular decision saw a little girl allowed through the cordon to place a kiss on the cheek of one of the disabled men travelling in the cars at the rear of the parade.

Back at the Palace, the relatives and other guests were assembled on the lawn, facing the West Terrace as the King and Queen and other members of the Royal family stepped out onto the balcony. Before them lay dense crowds of cheering spectators and suddenly, as the parade turned the corner to enter the Mall, the noise became deafening. What a sight that must have been for Gus, a farmer's son from a small Staffordshire village and how proud Cissy would surely have been to be able to witness for herself the esteem in which her husband and his fellow VCs were held by a grateful and grieving nation.

Once inside the Palace gates, the parade was brought to a halt and the order given to fall in to their allotted section; the sections being arranged in order of each announcement of the award of a VC in the 'London Gazette.' In front of Gus was Private W.B. Butler of the West Yorkshire Regiment and behind him Ernest Pitcher. In August 1917 Private Butler had picked up a shell from his trench and was just about to throw it when he noticed a group of men walking past. He shouted to them to hurry up and placed his body between the men and the shell, waiting until they were clear before throwing the shell which exploded immediately it left his hand.

The King, Prince Albert (the future King George VI) and other members of the Royal Party inspected the assembled ranks of men whose 'Gazette' dates spanned more than sixty years; then came the time for the individual presentations. Gus and his fellow VCs had been given a card showing their names, rank, date of the action in which their VC had been earned and their 'London Gazette' date. With the Royal family and other invited guests (including Field-Marshall Earl Haig and Secretary of State for War, Winston Churchill) assembled on the steps, the presentations began: each man stepping forward in turn and presenting his card before being received by the King and Queen. Sir Dighton Probyn was first in line and it must have been a very moving sight to see him and several other elderly and infirm VCs, leave their invalid chairs for a few moments in order to stand in front of their Sovereign. Equally moving was the presentation of those who had been blinded in the service of their country and the sight of wives, mothers, fathers and children watching the proceedings from the lawn whilst wearing their loved one's VC on their right breast. For them, the pride which they felt to be part of such an occasion, was surely eclipsed by the absence of their husband, son or father, and thoughts of what might have been.

With the formalities over, Gus joined Cissy on the lawn, enjoying a buffet of sandwiches, cake, strawberries and cream. The Band of the Welsh Guards, who had entertained them during lunch at the

Shipmates and friends.
Gordon Campbell and Gus
at Buckingham Palace.
Gus is wearing his VC and DSC.
His wound stripe, earned on
'Dunraven', is clearly visible on
his left sleeve.
(Courtesy of Stephen Snelling.)

barracks and then led the parade through the streets, played popular tunes for the rest of the afternoon. The Royal Party also took some refreshment before meeting with some of the families of those men who had not lived to witness the event. They included children, proudly wearing the medals of a father they had barely known, and parents clutching photos of their hero sons: anxious to get an opportunity to show them to the King.

Although such a gathering was inevitably tinged with some sadness, the overwhelming atmosphere was happy and informal. The nation faced serious problems in 1920, with many of those present struggling to find employment because of the economic depression. One newspaper even suggested that employers were particularly reluctant to employ war heroes because their temperament rendered them unsuitable for civilian employment. But, for a few hours on that June afternoon, children played on the lawn, adults chatted, enjoyed the refreshment, music and company and collected one another's autographs, whilst the King and Queen strolled around chatting to the informal groups.

At 18.00 the event drew to a close and, after signing autographs at the gate, Gus and his fellow VCs made their way home. It would be another nine years before they all met up again but, for many who were in attendance, Saturday 26th June 1920 was a day which would live long in their memories.

THE LAST LETTER.

Amongst Gus' personal papers is a seemingly insignificant letter, written by his father, Sam, to his son Gordon. It was written in December 1922 and Sam begins by telling his grandson, now aged four, that his pony is getting very slow and he thinks that he might need to get a new one. He then goes on to tell Gordon that his cousin, Michael, has had a bad cold but very much hopes to be back at school in time for the Christmas play in which he was playing the part of a pixie. He also informed him that another relative was thinking of having electric lights in the house and that his Aunt Mary had bought a motorcycle, something Sam was not at all happy about. It is not the content of the letter which is particularly significant but the date on which it was written: December 10th. It would appear that the letter was kept

Sam Bonner at the rear of Manor Farm. His three daughters, Mary, Dolly, and Kitty are also in the photograph which was taken around 1901.

amongst seemingly more important letters and documents, because it was very important to Gus. Seven days after he wrote the letter to his grandson, Sam Bonner died suddenly at the age of sixty-seven.

In an obituary in a local newspaper, Sam Bonner was described as being a 'typical farmer' in appearance: sturdy, bearded and more than six feet in height. Two years earlier, failing health had seen him give up his eight hundred acre farm (one of the largest in South Staffordshire) and go into semi-retirement, although he still farmed a much smaller plot of forty acres. While Sam Bonner's appearance might have been described as that of a typical farmer, the rest of his life was far from typical. As well as being one of the biggest employers in the district, he also found time to serve as the Aldridge representative on the Walsall Rural District Council (of which he was chairman for several years), as a Justice of the Peace and as a member of the Walsall Board of Guardians. He was a member of Aldridge Parish Council and an active supporter of local clubs and organisations, particularly the cricket and hockey clubs. It is a common misconception that Bonner Grove in Aldridge was named in honour of Gus but it was, in fact, named in honour of his father.

THE IDAHO.

During the 1920's Gus built a successful career as a well respected salvage expert and in 1929 he once again found himself making headlines in a number of newspapers; headlines such as, 'Triumph for salvage expert' and 'Idaho re-floated. Operations directed by VC.' The headlines were accompanied by photographs of both Gus and the ship, with the operation to re-float the *Idaho* even becoming the subject of several newspaper cartoons!

The Ellerman liner *Idaho* (4887 tons) had been on a voyage from Hull to New York with a large cargo of flour and oil when she attempted to enter Aberdeen harbour during a dense fog. Owing to her tonnage and the heavy seas, it proved impossible for the local tugs to keep her on course and, as a result, she ended up firmly stuck on Aberdeen beach. For more than six months she sat there, drawing crowds of sightseers, as first a local firm and then a salvage team from Newcastle attempted to re-float her. Newspaper reports of the time show that very little progress was made until Gus, with his crew and the salvage tug *Bullger*, took over the operation in May. Even so, it would take almost three months of patient work and skill before she could be removed.

The scale of the task which faced Gus and his team in their efforts to re-float the 'Idaho' can be clearly seen in this photograph dated 1st May 1929.

The method which Gus employed was said to be an object lesson in the practical application of hydrostatics; it was the power of the water which had caused the ship to be beached and it was the power of the water which re-floated her. Parts of the ship were deliberately flooded, whilst other parts were pumped out; the aim being to manoeuvre the ship into the best possible position to take advantage of the tide. On one occasion the salvage crew managed to move the ship 175ft but, on other occasions only a foot or two of progress was made. The operation very nearly failed due to calm seas and sandbanks but finally, after eleven weeks, Gus and his team managed to re-float her, towing her into Aberdeen harbour.

A remarkable piece of perseverance and skill saw the 'Idaho' re-floated in July 1929.

The *Idaho* had been stuck on the beach for seven months, becoming not just an item of interest and speculation for the locals but also a tourist attraction. Holidaymakers came especially to see it, with day-trippers from Glasgow swelling their numbers. Indeed, one newspaper editorial objected to the *Idaho* being moved, saying that she had given pleasure to thousands whilst she was stuck and that the only pleasure anyone would get from her now was the pleasure of those who were set to make money out of her. The editorial ended by suggesting that if the *Idaho* had to be salvaged, then the operation could have at least waited until the autumn when the tourist season had finished! It could however be argued that Gus and his crew did do their bit to benefit the Aberdeen tourism industry, with thousands of people watching the final days of the efforts to re-float her and raising a loud cheer when the *Idaho's* bows finally responded to the heaving waves. With estimated profits for the salvage company in excess of £10,000, the spectators were not the only people raising a cheer!

THE VC REUNION.

In the autumn of 1929, Gus received an invitation to a reunion of VCs which was to be held in London from November 9th to 11th. The reunion included a Dinner at the House of Lords to be hosted by the Prince of Wales (the future Edward VIII), tickets for the theatre, and a parade and service at the Cenotaph. Whereas the 1920 garden party had been organised in a hurry, organisation for the reunion was much more efficient, resulting in the attendance of almost three-quarters of the world's surviving VCs. The official guest list shows that all of the Q-ship VCs had accepted the invitation, as had Alan Jerrard, Gus' fellow VC from Bishop Vesey's School and Cecil Kinross, an old boy from Gus' other school, Coleshill.

Private Kinross was serving with the Canadian Expeditionary Force when he was awarded the VC for an action at Passchendaele in which he charged an enemy machine-gun post, killing the crew and destroying the gun.

His Royal Highness The Prince of Wales, Patron,
Admiral of the Fleet Earl Jellicoe, President,
and the
National Executive Council of the British Legion,
request the pleasure of the company of
C. G. Bonner Esq. V.C.
at a Dinner to be given in the Royal Gallery of the House of Lords
on November 9th at 7.30 p.m.
to recipients of the Victoria Cross.

R.S.V.P. to
Captain W. G. Willcox.
18. South Street.
Park Lane, London, W.1.

Lounge Suits.
Medals.

*Gus' invitation
to the VC Dinner,
9th November 1929.*

For several weeks before the event, newspapers carried lists of those who had confirmed their attendance, Gus being one of the first to accept. Twenty-eight made the long journey from Canada, whilst forty-five Australian VCs who were not able to make the trip, were entertained by the Governor-General in Australia. The main purpose of the event was to highlight the plight of ex-servicemen, widows and dependants. Donations to the Earl Haig Fund had grown year on year but, with their advancing years, many ex-servicemen were feeling the effects of their wartime experiences and needed increased financial assistance. It was hoped that the interest generated by the VC reunion would bring in those much needed funds.

In keeping with the spirit of the Victoria Cross, the only allocated seat at the Dinner on Saturday 9th November was for the Prince of Wales himself: all other places being decided by ballot. Gus, who was drawn as number 392 of 396 (the numbers including the gentlemen of the Press), shared a table with men of all ranks including a colonel and rear-admiral as well as privates and corporals. Adding to the informality was the absence of uniforms, with the order of the day being lounge suits and medals. By now only one of Gus' former comrades, Gordon Campbell, was still in the Navy. Ronald Stuart was pursuing a very successful career with Canadian Pacific, William Williams still lived and worked on Anglesey, Ernest Pitcher had retired from the Navy after twenty-five years service and Harold Auten lived in America, working for the Rank Organisation.

The reunion dinner was scheduled to begin at 19.30 but even those who arrived very early were cheered and applauded by the large crowd which had already gathered outside the Houses of Parliament. The VCs were to file through the Princes Chamber to be greeted by the Prince, before taking their seats in the Gallery. For a few moments it was just like the old days: four brave men led by their equally brave captain, as Gordon Campbell led his men, Stuart, Williams, Pitcher and Gus, to be received by the Prince.

An excellent dinner and a table laden with champagne, wine, whisky, cigars and cigarettes helped to create a relaxed atmosphere, as did the music provided by the string band of the Grenadier Guards, particularly the item on the programme entitled 'Tommies Tunes.' The speeches were kept short and to the point. Lord Jellicoe began by reading an appeal, signed by many of the VCs, for the public to help ex-servicemen and their dependants by the purchase of a Flanders poppy. The Prince was greeted with a loud and prolonged cheer and a chorus of 'For he's a jolly good fellow,' when he stood up to propose the toast. He spoke of his pride to be amongst such men, and of his sadness that the number present at the gathering would have been much larger had not so many men lost their lives whilst earning their VC and since. He also spoke of the many men denied the VC through lack of witnesses to their valour and those whose minds had been broken by the ordeals of war. On a lighter note, he joked that while he and many others might describe the award of the VC in terms such as valour, self-sacrifice, heroism and courage, the holders of the coveted bronze cross were more likely to describe their actions as simply an act of self-preservation or as an attempt to impress their commanding officer!

THE V.C. DINNER.

November 9th, 1929.

Notes for the information of all recipients of Victoria Cross.

To assist the British Legion in making the arrangements in London for the comfort of those attending the V.C. Dinner, it is asked that the following notes be carefully read, and the enclosed questionnaire answered and returned at the earliest possible date.

PROGRAMME. It is hoped that all attending the Dinner will be willing to remain in London for the other ceremonies which are being arranged, brief particulars of which are as follows:

> **Saturday November 9th.**—Dinner, Royal Gallery of House of Lords at 7.30 p.m.
>
> **Sunday November 10th.**—Special Evening performance of the play "Journey's End" at the Prince of Wales Theatre.
>
> **Monday November 11th.**—Service and Cenotaph Parade in morning.
>
> Festival of Remembrance at Royal Albert Hall in Evening.

RAILWAY TICKETS. The Railway Companies have agreed to provide free Rail Tickets for those V.C.'s who cannot meet this expense from their own resources. Those desiring to avail themselves of this offer must fill in the enclosed "Ticket Application Form" and return it without delay to **Captain W. G. Willcox, 18, South Street, London, W**, with the questionnaire, when the necessary tickets will be obtained and forwarded.

ACCOMMODATION IN LONDON. No doubt there will be many who will have no relatives or friends in London with whom they can stay, or who will not themselves be able to meet the expenses of accommodation and other incidentals. The British Legion has a special fund from which assistance can be provided, and it is hoped there will be no diffidence on the part of guests to state plainly on the questionnaire just what their needs are. The Legion can arrange accommodation if desired, and will notify all details to those concerned prior to their departure from their homes.

DRESS FOR THE DINNER. By the wish of H. R. H. The Prince of Wales, the dinner is to be marked by an absence of formality, and for this reason the general order will be lounge suits— with medals. Further, either light or dark lounge suits may be worn. If there is any special difficulty in this connection, please see questions Nos. 7/8 on attached form.

It should be particularly noted that all information given in reply to the questionnaire will be regarded as strictly confidential.

NOTE.—After receipt of completed questionnaire, further detailed particulars will be forwarded.

A letter containing information about the VC weekend in 1929.

Sunday was a free day but on that evening many of the VCs who had attended the House of Lords dinner were treated to a special performance of the play 'Journey's End' at the Prince of Wales Theatre. Gus and his fellow VCs were applauded by a large crowd as they arrived but quite what Gus - or Cissy for that matter - would have made of the many women amongst the crowd who were determined that they were going to steal a kiss from a VC, can only be guessed at. At the end of the performance, the audience stood and cheered until the author of the play came on stage to take a bow. Gus used the back page of his programme to acquire a few autographs, the first of which was William Williams, the man who had served with him on all three of his Q-ships.

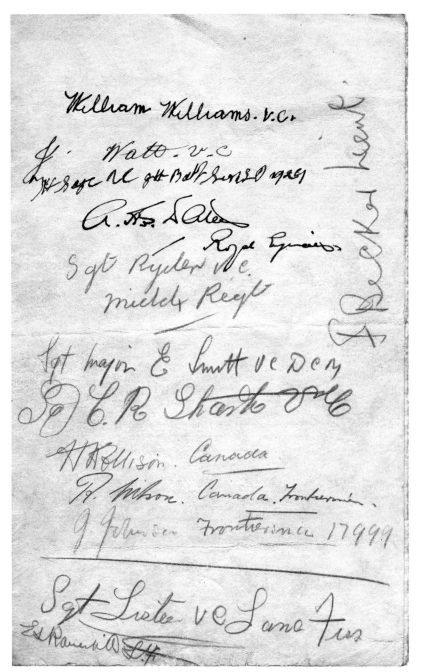

Gus used the back of his theatre programme to obtain the autographs of his fellow VCs, including the man who had served with him on all three of his Q-ships: William Williams VC DSM.

Whilst the VCs were at the theatre and through the night, an endless procession of people came to the cenotaph to lay wreaths and pay their respects. At midnight the poppy sellers took to the streets with their poppies, Lady Haig arriving at 6.00 to offer her thanks and encouragement.

After breakfast on Monday 11th November the VCs met up for a third time but this was to be a much more sombre occasion. The streets of London were lined with thousands of people for this, the eleventh Armistice Day parade and, at 10.20 and to the strains of 'Keep the Home Fires Burning,' the VCs took their place in the march to the Cenotaph. Some propelled themselves along in wheelchairs and one blind VC was led by his young daughter but all were determined to pay their respects to the dead and, hopefully, raise awareness of the plight of the living. Meanwhile, in Westminster Abbey, it must have been very moving to see so many women amongst the congregation wearing the medals of their husband, father or son as they filed past the tomb of the Unknown Warrior.

Millions of people throughout the world would never know where the body of their loved one lay. Some might get the opportunity to travel to France, Flanders or further afield to witness the name of their relative recorded on one of the memorials to the dead at places such as Thiepval or the Menin Gate. For many others, the tomb of the Unknown Warrior, containing as it does the remains of a serviceman from one of the European battlefields, became the focus of their grief. The VCs sent a wreath of laurel leaves and poppies which was laid at the tomb; the message on the card reading, 'Your sacrifice calls us to remembrance.'

During the afternoon, the VCs returned to the Cenotaph to lay their own wreaths and pay their private respects, whilst in the evening they attended the 'British Legion Festival of Empire and Remembrance' at the Royal Albert Hall. The evening began with the singing of the National Anthem, after which first the VCs and then the Chelsea Pensioners marched into the hall. The programme of music was long and varied, including popular and patriotic songs along with traditional marches. A rather unusual instruction in the programme concerned the welcome which was to be given to the Prince of Wales. It read:

> "When rising to acclaim His Royal Highness The Prince of Wales,
> the audience is requested to wave the programme (closed to show
> the coloured cover) high in the air."

While many of the people who had attended the VC weekend went home with happy memories and souvenir programmes, Gus and Cissy went back to Edinburgh with a little bit more. Several large poppy wreaths in the shape of a Victoria Cross had been made to decorate the House of Lords for the reunion and, after the meal, Gus enquired as to what they intended to do with them. As they had no firm plans, Gus asked whether he might be allowed to take one home with him. Whether he had actually given any thought as to how they were going to get their luggage and a large Victoria Cross onto the train is not known! However, the cross did arrive safely at Netherby Road; Gus deciding to have it made into a fire screen as a permanent reminder of a memorable day. Some years after his death, the screen was donated to the Royal British Legion Poppy Factory and is still on display in their museum along with an explanation as to its origins.

MORE HEADLINES.

In June 1930, Gus was involved in the salvage of the coal carrier SS *Beauport* which had been wrecked on the Agenor Rocks near St Peter Port, Guernsey. Crowds lined the foreshore and pleasure-craft watched as Gus and his team onboard the *Bullger*, used two submarines to act as pontoons thereby lifting the *Beauport* in what one newspaper described as 'an underwater trapeze.' As well as the journalists and photographers who were there to record the event, a gentleman called Mr Bennet was in attendance to obtain:

> "A permanent, moving record of this unique incident with his
> cinematograph."

A month later, Gus was asked if he would be the speaker at the Rotary Club lunch on the island, his subject being marine salvage. He told his audience that there were two basic methods of re-floating a ship: copper damming or the use of pontoons. Copper damming involved building up a ship to the water level and pumping out, whilst the pontoon method required a diver to place light lines under the vessel and then the use of heavy hawsers drawn under and fastened to the sunken pontoons. The pontoons would then be emptied of water and, as they came to the surface, so did the vessel. It is possible to begin to understand the huge costs involved in salvage operations when it becomes feasible to use submarines as pontoons as Gus had done in raising the *Beauport*. A newspaper report of the salvage described Gus as:

Despite his busy career, Gus did manage some free time.
This family holiday snap, taken in the early 1930's shows him sitting, second left.
The young man in front of him is the writer of the foreword to this book: David Partridge.

" quiet and unassuming, yet controlling with a masterly ability."

A stark reminder of how dangerous a job salvage work could be came in November 1934 when Gus and his crew were involved in the salvage of the Icelandic trawler *Geysir* which had run on the rocks at Torness Point; her crew of seventeen men and one woman being rescued by the Longhope lifeboat. Gus and his crew of fourteen worked for thirty-six hours in wild weather and dangerous seas until, eventually, their efforts paid off and the trawler was re-floated. Six members of the crew went on board the ship in order to pump water from her, while Gus and the rest of his men were towing from the *Bullger*. All was going well, despite the terrible conditions, until suddenly, after being towed for two and a half hours and without warning, the timbers of the *Geysir* began to come apart and she started to sink. Gus described what happened next:

> "There were eighty fathoms of steel rope between the two boats. We in
> the tug saw the frantic signalling of our mates. We realised immediately
> their danger. The trawler was sinking rapidly. We slipped the towing
> rope without a seconds delay and raced back to the *Geysir* and drew
> alongside. Despite the heavy seas that were running, the men aboard
> jumped across the space between the two boats, and we raced away
> from the sinking wreck. Within three minutes of the first sign of danger
> she had disappeared beneath the water."

In November 1935, a number of newspapers, including 'The Times,' reported on the operations to re-float the Marius Nelson steamer *Elizabeth* from a reef at Johnstones' Point, Campbeltown. The *Elizabeth* had been on the rocks for more than a month, having been grounded in a south-westerly gale and her crew being

The salvage tug 'Bullger.'

rescued with the help of local people who were willing to brave the dreadful weather. When the ship's captain and chief engineer managed to board the vessel two days later, they found her firmly lodged on the reef but, in what the newspapers described as a remarkable feat of seamanship, Gus and the crew of the *Bullger* managed to re-float her; towing her to Campbeltown to the cheers of the very large crowd who had gathered to watch the event. They were also able to witness a further feat of seamanship as the ship was skilfully berthed in a harbour basin which was only a few feet longer than herself. The '*Cambeltown Courier*' reported that it had been one of the most remarkable salvage feats recorded in the history of such operations around Britain.

SAD NEWS.

Earlier in 1935, Gus and Cissy had received the sad news that his mother, Jane, had died at the age of seventy-seven. During her lifetime Jane Bonner had not only found time to raise five children and help her husband to run Manor Farm, she had also been associated with many social and charitable causes in Aldridge. She had been a founder member of the Aldridge and District Nursing Association, was vice-chairman of the Women's Institute, been involved in the Aldridge Welfare Centre, the Mothers Union and the Hockey Club as well as being a visitor and collector for local charities. During the Great War she worked tirelessly in raising funds for the Manor House Hospital which stood next to Manor Farm and provided much needed care for recovering servicemen. And, of course, Jane found time to write the weekly letters to her family which have been such a valuable source for this book, not just of factual information but of personal perspective and opinion.

Chief mourners at her funeral were Gus and Cissy, her daughters Kitty and Dolly and Kitty's husband Bert (Partridge). Her eldest son, Samuel, was still living in Canada and, following the death of his wife in 1929, his sister Mary had emigrated there where she worked as a nurse whilst also supporting her brother in raising his three daughters. As well as her five children, Jane was survived by six grandchildren and one great-grandson, Walter Edward Bonner McCallum the son of Jane's oldest grandchild, Catherine Lees McCallum nee Bonner. Jane was buried with her husband in the churchyard of Aldridge Parish Church.

FURTHER HONOURS.

In 1937, Gus was informed that he had been chosen to receive the Coronation Medal which was being issued to 90,000 recipients from all walks of life to commemorate the coronation of King George V1. The medal was of silver, the obverse showing the crowned heads of the King and Queen and the reverse showing the royal cypher.

TWO VCS IN ALDRIDGE.

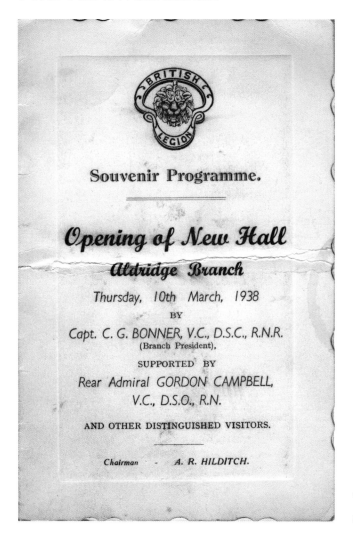

The front page of the souvenir programme for the opening of the British Legion Hall in 1938.

1938 saw Gus back in Aldridge for the opening of the new British Legion Hall on March 10th. As president of the branch since its founding in 1928, Gus had been invited to officially open the hall and, as well as welcoming their own VC, the people of Aldridge were very pleased to welcome Gordon Campbell who had by now left the Navy, served as a Member of Parliament and was a successful author and lecturer.

In officially declaring the hall open, Gus spoke of his great pleasure in being able to renew old acquaintances in Aldridge, expressing his thanks to the chairman and secretary for their hard work in establishing what was a very successful branch of the British Legion in Aldridge. Throughout the evening a varied programme of musical entertainment was on offer, as was a most appetising menu which included tomato soup, roast pork and a sweet of blackcurrant tart and custard.

When the time came for Gordon Campbell's address, he took the opportunity to praise his former crew, those who had lost their lives in the war and - much to Gus' embarrassment - his former first officer! Referring to the many medals which he had been awarded in his illustrious career, he said that they were entirely due to the fact that he had had the good fortune to:

"Command the finest crew that ever sailed God's seas."

His comments about Gus were greeted with thunderous applause. He said:

"I have seen my first lieutenant, Captain Bonner, sitting on top of the deck, getting red hot, and with the ship on fire and immediately underneath him was a magazine which he knew must be blown up. In my opinion, Captain Bonner is the bravest man I ever met."

The opening of the British Legion Hall, Aldridge.
Gus is standing, second left. Gordon Campbell is standing fourth left.
(Courtesy of the Walsall Observer.)

Campbell then paid tribute to those who had lost their lives in the Great War, saying that many of them had accomplished deeds which deserved the VC, "a dozen times over."

The end of his speech was reserved not for the war which had gone but the one which was to come. For many years Britain and much of the world had been surveying the political situation in Germany with growing unease and as the storm clouds began to gather, Britain made preparations for a war which, for many, seemed inevitable. As early as 1935 the Government had issued its first leaflet on air-raid precautions, whilst 1936 saw a pledge of more than a million pounds to provide gas masks for the entire population. Gordon Campbell spoke of the variety of recruiting appeals which were being made by the armed forces, suggesting that a direct appeal would be more effective. "Why," he asked, "Do we not just say to our young men, join up and do something for your country and defend its freedom."

In September 1939, when the Second World War began, neither Gus nor Gordon Campbell could be considered young men but, at the age of fifty-three and at the request of his old friend Winston Churchill,

Gordon Campbell came out of retirement to serve his country again, as did Ernest Pitcher. For Gus, at the age of fifty-four, the war years would see him serve his country again; not by waging war himself but by utilising the skills he had acquired during his salvage career to provide vital raw materials for the war effort. And, like thousands of parents who had lived through the horrors of the First World War, Gus and Cissy would soon see their only son called to serve in the Second.

Opening of the British Legion Hall, Aldridge. Gus and Gordon Campbell are standing at the top table,
easily identified by the number of medals they wear.
(Courtesy of the Walsall Observer.)

Chapter 9
SERVICE TO THE END

War came early to Edinburgh; the area's association with shipping making it a prime target for Hitler's bombers. Less than six weeks after the declaration of hostilities, Cissy wrote to her sister-in-law, Kitty, regarding an air-raid for which the people of the city had received no warning other than a German radio broadcast which had said that although Edinburgh was a beautiful city, it wouldn't stay that way for long. Cissy said that there had been no siren or warning of any kind; people on the streets looking to the skies and believing that they were watching a very realistic air-raid practice! Not until a German plane flew low enough over the roof-tops for people to be able to see its markings and the bullets passing between it and a British plane, did people realise that it was a real air-raid. Gus was in his office at the time and, when he came out for a cup of tea, someone said to him:

> "I thought those planes were going to hit me. Thank God they were
> not Germans!"

Surgeon-Lieutenant Gordon Dunraven Bonner.

Not only were they enemy aircraft but they had narrowly missed ships in the harbour before crash landing in the sea. The events which Cissy described would go down in history as the first air-raid on Britain in the Second World War. On Monday 16th October 1939, approximately twelve Junkers JU88 flew over the Forth area. Their purpose was not mentioned in the official report but it was suggested that they had spotted the battleship HMS *Hood* heading towards the Forth. Others have suggested it was just a general raid on shipping in the area, with several ships at Rosyth being attacked, although none were badly damaged. Gus had been attempting to raise a dredger in Rosyth but had come home because he needed a piece of equipment and was due to return the next day. Sadly, fifteen men were killed at Rosyth on that Monday afternoon and twelve seriously injured; had Gus not come home he may have been one of them.

The official report shows that four German planes were brought down and, within a few days, Edinburgh was to witness some unusual scenes as the bodies of two young German air-men were buried. Overnight their coffins - draped in the German flag and complete with swastikas - rested in St Peters Church and on Friday 20th October crowds lined the streets to pay their respects, as did a guard of sixty men of the RAF. Adding to the sombre atmosphere, a piper played a highland lament.

Gus and Cissy's son Gordon was training to be a doctor at the outbreak of war and was in a lecture at the time of the raid. The professor who was giving the lecture was very safety conscious and had made his students practice air-raid procedures on several occasions. However the lack of a warning siren seemed to have lulled him into a false sense of security, as when the students voiced their concerns to him that this seemed to be a real air-raid, he ignored them and continued with his lecture!

On completion of his medical training at Edinburgh University and the Edinburgh Royal Infirmary in 1941, Gordon Dunraven Bonner joined the RNVR as a Surgeon-Lieutenant. It was whilst he was serving at the commando training base near Spean Bridge that he met a young Wren called Pam who was to be his future wife. He went on to serve in the Far East.

THE WAR EFFORT.

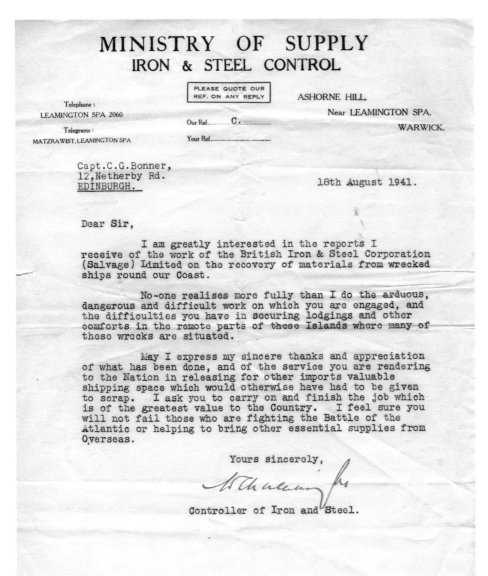

A letter of thanks for the service which Gus rendered to the nation in the Second World War.

In August 1940, Gus left the Leith Salvage and Towage Company after twenty-one years service, taking up a new position with the British Iron and Steel Corporation (Salvage) Limited, Ministry of Supply, BISCO for short. For the purpose of salvaging metal for the war effort, the Ministry had divided the British Isles into twelve areas, with Gus being appointed chief salvage officer for the Forth area. Not only was he very successful, as one might expect from someone who had been involved in commercial salvage for more than twenty years, but the operations under his command turned out to be extremely cost efficient. Official records show that during the first year of his employment he salvaged more metal than any salvage officer in the country and, in the quarter ending March 1941, operations under his command yielded 3,195 tons whilst the remaining eleven areas recovered just 3,703 between them. BISCO's returns for the period 1940-42 show that Gus salvaged 13,140 tons, putting the Forth region in overall second place behind Mersey and North Wales with ninety-six tons more. However, as mentioned in a previous chapter, the key to a good salvage operation was not just the recovery of a ship and its cargo but also the costs involved in doing so. At just 61/- per ton in direct costs (£3.05), Gus' area was the most cost efficient: Mersey and North Wales spending almost twice as much per ton and the most expensive region more than seven times as much on recovery as the Forth area had.

During the war years, Gus also found time to serve as a member of Number 5 Battalion, 'D' Company, Edinburgh Home Guard. In a letter written after Gus' death, Cissy told Gordon that his father had been awarded a medal for his service in the Home Guard. The medal is likely to have been the Defence Medal 1939-45, one of the qualifying criteria being three years service in the Home Guard.

In what little spare time Gus had between his salvage work for the war effort and his Home Guard duties, Gus enjoyed bowling and also joined the Royal Forth Yacht Club. The restrictions brought about by the war meant that the club was mainly a social club, but no doubt Gus would have enjoyed spending a few hours socialising with others who shared his love of the sea.

THE BIGGEST SHIP EVER SALVAGED.

In 1943, Gus and his team were responsible for the raising of the 56,000 ton naval training ship *Caledonia* in the Firth of Forth and, once again, Gus found his name and photograph in newspapers and magazines.

The *Caledonia* had begun life in Hamburg in 1913 as the German liner *Bismarck* and for more than twenty years she was the biggest ship in the world. She had been launched just before the Great War but never sailed under a German flag: the Treaty of Versailles awarding the ship to the White Star Line as reparation for their losses as a result of German attacks on their fleet. She was renamed RMS *Majestic* and became one of White Star's most popular ships, completing more than 200 voyages to New York in her illustrious career and being capable of carrying more than 2,000 passengers. She was finally laid-up in 1935 and sold for scrap to a company called T.W. Ward. The Admiralty, however, had other plans for her.

Under the terms of the agreement which saw the *Bismarck/Majestic* handed over as a prize of war, it was stipulated that she could not be sold to the Admiralty. However the Admiralty, no doubt after consulting the small print, offered T.W. Ward a swap which they accepted: twenty-four outmoded destroyers in exchange for the *Majestic*. Following her conversion the ship was re-commissioned in April 1937 as the naval training vessel HMS *Caledonia*, having accommodation for 2,000 young men. At the outbreak of war it was decided that it would be a wise precaution to move the cadets to shore bases; the *Caledonia* being temporarily anchored in the Firth of Forth while the Admiralty decided what to do with her. Unfortunately, matters were taken out of their hands when the *Caledonia* caught fire and sank into thirty feet of mud at the end of September 1939. Under the terms of the agreement between T.W. Ward and the

Admiralty, the firm was given first option on the ship. It was decided that a full-scale salvage operation in the Firth of Forth would attract too much attention from the German Luftwaffe and present the very real danger of the enemy attempting to sink the ship as she was being moved. This could have caused a hazard to shipping and so Wards opted to take only what they could easily remove. In July 1941 they informed the Admiralty that they had taken just 7,000 tons of metal from the ship and that they had no further use for her.

By 1943 Gus was a very successful and respected salvage officer but of all the vessels he had raised or re-floated, the raising of the *Caledonia* must rank as his greatest salvage success; not only was the actual act of salvaging the ship a testament to his skill and patience, but the value to the nation of more than 40,000 tons of high quality steel was immense. More than 1,800 portholes on the ship had to be painstakingly sealed before she could be pumped out and raised. Given the enormous size of the vessel - being more than twice the length of the pitch at the new Wembley stadium - it is a testament to all those involved in the huge operation that the *Caledonia* came up at the first attempt. Records suggest that the metal provided for the war effort by Gus and his crew was likely to be sufficient to build between twelve and twenty cruisers!

Newspapers of the time reported that the *Caledonia* was by far the biggest ship ever salvaged, describing the task as both formidable and:

"forming an outstanding page in the history of naval salvage."

A letter, which appears to be from a fellow salvage expert, reads:

"I thought that I would take the opportunity, now the *Caledonia* remains are at Inverkeithing, of tendering to you my personal congratulations on the completion of this exceptionally difficult operation. Such a large undertaking must of necessity have carried proportionately heavy anxieties, some of which we have shared in thought, if not in substance but on each occasion these have been removed by the successful performances achieved under your supervision. It has been a long job, but one which, on result, cannot but reflect the highest credit and afford you the fullest satisfaction. Although I am expressing these sentiments personally, I feel sure that they will be shared by all of us with an intimate knowledge of the problems attaching to this large project."

TIRPITZ.

During the years after the war had ended, Gus was involved with some of the most famous ships in the world. In July 1947 he was medically examined prior to being flown to Norway; being rated at the military rank of Major and charged with offering advice as to the possibility of salvaging the formidable German battleship, *Tirpitz*.

Winston Churchill had nicknamed the ship 'the Beast' and a beast she was: waiting in her 'lair' for an opportunity to pounce on her prey. The *Tirpitz* had a significant influence on the Second World War without actually doing very much. It was the threat of what she could do which occupied both the Navy and the RAF in trying to make sure that she did not break out into the open sea, whilst constantly trying to find a way of destroying her and thereby removing her latent menace. Many attempts were made to sink her until eventually, on a beautiful and calm Norwegian morning in 1944, Lancaster Bombers armed with tallboy bombs dealt her a devastating blow resulting in more than a thousand deaths and causing the *Tirpitz* to turn over, coming to rest upside down in the fjord. A measure of the power needed to finally end the ship's reign of terror - and thereby free precious resources of both ships, planes and men for other tasks - can be gauged from the capability of the tallboy bombs which were powerful enough to penetrate sixteen feet of concrete and were, therefore, considered capable of damaging the eight inch thick steel deck of the *Tirpitz*. The 'Beast' was destroyed at last.

During the ongoing operation to salvage the *Tirpitz*, a Norwegian salvage company found part of an engine-room door on which someone had painted the words 'gegen England' (against England). It was mounted and presented to the RAF with the inscription:

> "Part of the battleship *Tirpitz*, sunk by Nos 9 and 617 Squadrons 12th
> November 1944 at Tromso. Presented to Bomber Command by
> brothers-in-arms, Royal Norwegian Air Force in commemoration
> of friendship and co-operation during World War II."

THE END FOR SOME ICONIC BATTLESHIPS.

Gus, second left, on HMS 'Revenge.' the young man wearing glasses, far right, is his nephew, David Partridge.

Whilst still employed by BISCO, Gus was charged with supervising the delivery of some of the nation's biggest and best loved ships to breakers yards in Scotland, principally at Rosyth, Inverkeithing and Faslane. Foremost of these ships, in terms of their place in the public's affection, were HMS *Nelson* and HMS *Rodney*. When Parliament announced that the ships would be broken up in January 1948, tributes

HMS 'Revenge.'
Gus can be seen
far left with his
hands in his pockets.

were paid from the floor of the House to the role of these great ships in our nation's history; saying that both the officers and men who had served on them and the public in general, very much regretted their loss. Between them *Nelson* and *Rodney* had been involved in many of the major operations of the war, including the Normandy landings. Gus' career at sea had begun on small sailing ships such as the *Invermark* and the *Ashmore* and now, less than fifty years later, he found himself involved with the last voyages of these comparatively gigantic, powerful battleships.

The final journey
of HMS 'Rodney,'
a ship which had
a special place
in public affection.

*HMS 'Nelson' on her way
to the breakers yard.*

Gus was also responsible for supervising the delivery of the 28,000 ton battleship HMS *Revenge* - which had taken part in the Battle of Jutland during the Great War - and her sister ships, HMS *Resolution* and HMS *Royal Sovereign*. Throughout his life Gus had often faced danger: it being part of his chosen career. The only thing which is predictable about a life at sea is its unpredictability; no doubt that was part of the appeal. But having already brought several of the nation's battleships to the breakers yard, Gus would surely have viewed the delivery of HMS *Royal Sovereign* as just another job. However, it was the opinion of some members of his family, including Cissy, that it was an incident on that ship which contributed to Gus' illness and subsequent death.

CROSSING THE BAR.

During the years in which HMS *Royal Sovereign* had been on loan to the Russian Navy, eye-witness reports suggest that she had not been kept in a state which would be considered suitable by the British. Indeed, it was claimed that when she was returned to Britain in 1949 the men who were charged with the responsibility of her delivery to the breakers yard and subsequent breaking up, found her in such a filthy state that at the end of every day the overalls which they had worn whilst on-board were destroyed. At some stage during the operation, Gus was soaked in oil from the vessel and it was this drenching which Cissy believed caused his cancer. In June 1950 Gus had a lung removed, but sadly the cancer spread to his other lung and to his liver. His nephew, David Partridge, recalls that even in the last few days of his life Gus was his usual cheery self: sitting up in bed, smiling and chatting. Gus was, by now, a proud grandfather to

Stephen Dunraven Bonner who was almost four, and to Penelope who was nine months old. It is sad to think that Gus would never be able to share his experiences with his grandchildren in person but his family's amazing collection of photographs, newspaper cuttings, documents and letters ensures that his memory lives on.

Gus with his son Gordon and grandson Stephen.

12 Netherby Road, Edinburgh had been Gus' home for more than thirty years and it was here, at 6.00 on Wednesday February 7th 1951, that he died. Three days later he was cremated at Warriston Road Crematorium. He was sixty-six. The hymns which were chosen for the service were 'Sunset and Evening Star' (a favourite of naval men), the '23rd Psalm', and the wonderfully uplifting hymn: 'Praise My Soul the King of Heaven'. Several newspapers carried the news of his death, detailing some of the main points of what had been a very full life; one report beginning with Gordon Campbell's description of Gus as the bravest man he had ever met.

A month later Cissy made the long trip from Edinburgh to Staffordshire carrying her husband's ashes in an oak casket to his final resting place: the graveyard of Aldridge Parish Church, just a few hundred yards from his boyhood home, Manor Farm. Despite his many years at sea and in Scotland, Aldridge was the place which Gus called home and the people of the village were proud to honour one of their bravest sons with a procession through the village followed by a memorial service at the Parish Church. The procession included members of the council, the Staffordshire Regiment, representatives of the British Legion, the police force and the sea-cadets, as well as family and friends. They made their way past many of the places which had been part of Gus' life: the house in the High Street where he had lived when the family first moved to the village from Shuttington in 1885; the hall where he, Cissy and Jane had received such a wonderful reception following the award of his VC; the headquarters of the British Legion of which Gus had been president since it's formation in 1928; and, of course, Manor Farm where his parents had entertained a stream of press-men and well-wishers on the day after his visit to Sandringham in 1917.

On Saturday March 17th 1951, Gus' ashes were placed in a plot near to the entrance gate of the Aldridge graveyard; a large gathering of friends, family and local people looking on as eight members of the Staffordshire Regiment fired three volleys in his honour. Fittingly, for a man who was once a young cadet himself, Last Post and Reveille were played by a member of the sea-cadets. The inscription on his grave includes the words, 'Love Alone Is Eternal.'

CISSY.

Cissy returned to live in Scotland but her husband's bravery was not forgotten. In 1956 she received an invitation to represent Gus at a gathering in London to mark the 100th anniversary of the Victoria Cross but, sadly, only one of Gus' old pals from 'Campbell's Q-ships' was able to respond to the invitation in person. Ernest Pitcher, Gus' fellow *Dunraven* VC had died of tuberculosis in 1946, having once again volunteered to serve his country in the Second World War and having had several occupations during the inter-war years. Ronald Stuart, the elected VC on *Pargust* who had had a very successful career with Canadian Pacific, retired in 1951 and died three years later aged sixty-seven. To describe Gordon Campbell's life as eventful would be something of an understatement. Vice-Admiral, VC, author, ADC to the King, lecturer, Member of Parliament for Burnley and one of the most famous and popular naval men of the Great War. Yet his last years of serving his country in the Second World War were fraught with difficulties, ending with his retirement through ill-health in 1943. He died in October 1953 at the age of sixty-seven. Their old boss, Admiral Sir Lewis Bayly, whom Gus had stayed in touch with after the war, had died in 1936 at the age of seventy-nine.

Cissy was invited to represent her husband in the celebrations to mark the centenary of the Victoria Cross.

William Williams, the man who had held the gun-screens in place on the *Pargust* was the only one of Campbell's men who was able to respond to the 100th anniversary invitation in person. The people of Anglesey were rightly proud of the man they called 'Will VC'. He died at his home in Holyhead in 1965 aged seventy-five and Anglesey has several memorials dedicated to this brave and popular man.

The service of thanksgiving on the occasion of the centenary of the institution of the Victoria Cross which Cissy attended as a representative of her late husband, was held at Westminster Abbey at 15.00 on Monday 25th June 1956 and on the following day the Queen held a review of the holders of the VC in Hyde Park. The official programme shows that both VCs from Gus' old schools - Alan Jerrard from Bishop Vesey's and Cecil Kinross from Coleshill - attended the gathering.

In 1967, Cissy received an invitation to the opening of the newly-built Aldridge Community Centre. After the official opening ceremony two plaques were unveiled: one by Mrs Stirling in honour of her husband Dr John Stirling who had been the first president of the Aldridge Central Community Association and a very respected local GP, and the second by Cissy in honour of Gus who was described in the programme as:

> "A well-known local figure in Aldridge in former times, who won the
> VC in the 1914-18 war."

One of the rooms in the centre was named as 'The VC Room' in his honour.

Cissy returned to live in Aldridge for a few years before moving for the final time to be nearer to her son Gordon and his family; Gordon having been a GP in March, Cambridgeshire, since 1949. She died at St Johns Hospital, Peterborough on May 25th 1973 at the age of eighty.

LICHFIELD CATHEDRAL.

On 10th June 2007 several members of Gus' family, including his great-grandson, James Bonner and his nephew, David Partridge, attended a service of remembrance at Lichfield Cathedral celebrating the 150th anniversary of the institution of the Victoria Cross and the 50th anniversary of the Victoria Cross and George Cross Association. The citations for two local VCs were read out during the service and the roll of honour at the back of the order of service carried the names of fifty-six VC holders (including Gus) and twenty-one men who had won the George Cross, all of whom came from Midland counties.

AND FINALLY...

Gus Bonner was not born in Aldridge, nor did he die there. He had lived in Scotland for more than thirty years and spent many years at sea but, for Gus, Aldridge was the place he called home. In 1917, the year he won his Victoria Cross, Aldridge was a small Staffordshire village whose people were very proud that 'one of them' had shown bravery which had resulted in the award of the nation's 'badge of courage.' As the years have gone by, those who knew Gus personally have grown fewer and fewer and I am not sure that Aldridge schoolchildren are taught about their local hero in quite the same way I was when I went to school in the village in the 1960's. But Gus Bonner has not been forgotten: in fact 2008 has seen not only the publication of his biography but also the dedication of a memorial which honours his valour. The memorial, erected by Walsall Council in 2007, could hardly be in a more fitting position, standing as it does adjacent to the Aldridge War Memorial and opposite the site on which Manor Farm, his boyhood home, once stood.

On a warm and sunny afternoon, September 21st 2008, I joined a crowd of more than three hundred at

Aldridge War Memorial in the 1960's.
The building to the right of the photograph is Manor Farm: Gus' boyhood home.

the dedication service of the Bonner Memorial. As the parade of veterans and standards, led by the band of the Sutton Coldfield Sea Cadets, made their way to the memorial, the standards fluttered gently in the breeze and the sun glinted on the many medals on display, both in the parade and amongst the crowd. Four young men of the Sea Cadets stood at the corners of the memorial, their heads bowed, boots beautifully polished, resting on their rifles, as the service began with a prayer for the one hundred and one men whose names are recorded on the village's war memorial. The Rector of Aldridge, Reverend Richard Cornfield,

Another view of the War Memorial in 2008 showing the Bonner Memorial to the right of the picture,
set within the surrounding wall.
(Courtesy of John Hunt.)

127

IN MEMORY OF

CAPT. CHARLES GEORGE BONNER ("GUS")

V.C., D.S.C., R.N.R.

1884 - 1951

AN ALDRIDGE MAN AWARDED

THE VICTORIA CROSS

FOR CONSPICUOUS GALLANTRY IN ACTION

WITH AN ENEMY SUBMARINE

ON BOARD HMS DUNRAVEN

8TH AUGUST 1917

The plaque on the Bonner Memorial.

and Royal British Legion chaplain Reverend Martin C. Rutter, vicar of St Margaret's Church, Great Barr, led the service which included prayers, a reading, the dedication of the memorial and the singing of three hymns: 'O God Our Help in Ages Past,' 'Jerusalem' and 'Eternal Father Strong to Save. A particularly moving sight towards the end of the service was to see some of the veterans struggling to their feet, some with the help of sticks, in order to stand for a few moments for the singing of the National Anthem.

At the end of the service the Mayor of Walsall, Councillor Tom Ansell, who had laid a wreath at the memorial, spoke of Walsall's pride in its VCs. David Partridge, Gus' nephew who was himself a captain in India and Burma during the Second World War, thanked everyone for attending and also paid tribute to Walsall Council for erecting the memorial to his uncle. The Member of Parliament for Aldridge/Brownhills, Richard Shepherd, spoke for only a brief time but his words were both meaningful and totally appropriate for the occasion and resulted in loud and spontaneous applause. Mr Shepherd paid tribute to Gus and all of those who had served their country in war, particularly the men of the village who had paid the ultimate price: those whose names were carved on the memorial behind him. In a year which has seen the publication of this biography, the dedication of the Bonner Memorial and the completion of the refurbishment of the Aldridge War Memorial, it seems entirely fitting to complete this book with the words which Mr Shepherd chose to end his speech:

"LEST WE FORGET."

Selected Bibliography

Pull Together: The Memoirs of Admiral Sir Lewis Bayly. George G. Harrap, 1934

Q-Boat Adventures. Lieut. Comm. Harold Auten VC. Herbert Jenkins, 1919.

Q-ships and their Story. E. Keble Chatterton. Conway Maritime Press, 1972

Danger Zone. The Story of the Queenstown Command. E. Keble Chatterton. Rich and Cowan, 1934.

Smoke and Mirrors. Deborah Lake. Sutton Publishing, 2006

My Mystery Ships. Rear-Admiral Gordon Campbell VC, DSO. First published in Great Britain in 1928 by Hodder and Stoughton. Republished by Periscope Publishing Ltd, 2002.

The Life of a Q-Ship Captain. The Autobiography of Rear-Admiral Gordon Campbell VC DSO. First published in Great Britain in1932 under the title of 'Number Thirteen' by Hodder and Stoughton. Republished by Periscope Publishing Ltd, 2002.

Q-Ships. Carson Ritchie. Terence Dalton, 1985.

VCs Of The First World War. The Naval VCs. Stephen Snelling. Sutton Publishing, 2002.

Victoria Cross Heroes. Michael Ashcroft. Headline Publishing Group, 2006.

A Party Fit For Heroes. Derek Hunt and John Mulholland. The Naval and Military Press Ltd, 2007.

Battle Beneath The Waves. U-Boats At War. Robert C. Stern. Castle Books, 2003.

Walsall Serviceman 1914-18 A Guide To Research. Sue Satterthwaite. Walsall Local History Centre, 1998.

Leaving The Village. Sue Satterthwaite. Walsall Local History Centre, 2005.

The Tirpitz. David Woodward. William Kimber and Co Ltd, 1955.

The Medals Year Book. Token Publishing Ltd, 1993.

Last of the Windjammers. Volume 1. Basil Lubbock. James Brown and Son, 1927.

Last of the Windjammers. Volume 2. Basil Lubbock. James Brown and Son, 1935.

Liddell Hart's History Of The Great War. Liddell Hart. Book Club Associates, 1973

The First World War. John Keegan. Hutchinson, 1998

Aldridge History Trail. Betty Fox. Walsall Local History Centre, 1990

An Account Of The Motor Vessel Eilian. Peter Newcombe. 2008.

HMS Conway 1859-1974. Alfie Windsor. Witherbys Publishing and Seamanship International, 2008.

Newspapers and Periodicals

Daily Sketch; Daily Mail; Daily Express; London Gazette; The Times; Boston Herald; New York Times; Sunday Pictorial; Walsall Observer; Walsall Pioneer; Scottish Daily Mail; Daily Mirror; The Scotsman; Aberdeen Press and Journal; Sphere Magazine; Guernsey Evening Press; Guernsey Weekly Press; Royal Naval Division Magazine; Pearson's Magazine; Edinburgh Evening News; The Log (Furness Withy); *The Cadet* (HMS Conway); Magazine of Aldridge Parish Church; Kelly's Directory; various unidentified newspapers-England and Scotland.

Sources

Records of the Following

Aberdeen Art Gallery and Museums; Aldridge Parish Church; Amgueddfa Cymru -National Museum Wales; Anglesey County Record Office; Bishop Vesey's School; British Library. Newspapers; City of Edinburgh Council; Coleshill School; Cooper and Jordan School; Edinburgh University; Imperial War Museum, London; Fleet Air Arm Museum; Great War Medals Research Service; Guildhall Library (Ms 18570/1); Liverpool City Council Archives; Lloyds of London; Merseyside Maritime Museum; National Archives; National Archives of Scotland; The Royal Collection; Royal Forth Yacht Club; Royal Naval Submarine Museum; Tamworth Library; Walsall Local History Centre; United States Naval Historical Foundation.

Other Sources

Letters and personal papers of Gus, Cissy, Dolly, Jane and Samuel Bonner; letter's of Gordon Campbell, Lewis Bayly, William Sims and many others; Aunt Helen's Diary; Souvenir Programme of the Victoria Cross Centenary 1956; Programme for the VC Dinner 1929; Theatre programme 'Journey's End' 1929; an extract from Der *U-Bootskrieg 1914-18* by Vice-Admiral Andreas Michelsen which was sent to Gus Bonner. It has not been possible to confirm whether the extract was actually used in the final publication.

Websites

www.ancestry.co.uk
www.uboat.net
www.1914-18.invisionzone.com/forums
www.cwgc.org
www.nationalarchives.gov.uk
www.nytimes.com
www.victoriacrosssociety.com
www.naval-history.net/WW1NavyBritishQships.htm
www.mercantilemarine.org
www.raf.mod.uk
www.newcombe.info/index.htm
www.oxforddnb.com
www.hmsconway.org